AQUARIUS

21 JANUARY – 19 FEBRUARY

First published in Great Britain 2012
by Mills & Boon, an imprint of Harlequin (UK) Limited,
Eton House, 18-24 Paradise Road, Richmond, Surrey TW9 1SR

ISBN: 978 0 263 90262 4

Typeset by Midland Typesetters

Harlequin (UK) policy is to use papers that are natural, renewable and recyclable products and made from wood grown in sustainable forests. The logging and manufacturing processes conform to the legal environmental regulations of the country of origin.

Printed and bound in Spain
by Blackprint CPI, Barcelona

Dedicated to

The Light of Intuition

Sri V. Krishnaswamy—mentor and friend

With thanks to

Joram and Isaac

Special thanks to

Nyle Cruz for her creative input

and

Janelle Cook for editorial support

ABOUT DADHICHI

Dadhichi is one of Australia's foremost astrologers and is frequently seen on TV and in the media. He has the unique ability to draw from complex astrological theory to provide clear, easily understandable advice and insights for people who want to know what their future may hold.

In the 28 years that Dadhichi has been practising astrology, face reading and other esoteric studies, he has conducted over 10,000 consultations. His clients include celebrities, political and diplomatic figures, and media and corporate identities from all over the world.

Dadhichi's unique blend of astrology and face reading helps people fulfil their true potential. His extensive experience practising western astrology is complemented by his research into the theory and practice of eastern forms of astrology.

Dadhichi has been a guest on many Australian television shows and several of his political and worldwide forecasts have proved uncannily accurate. He appears regularly on Australian television networks and is a regular columnist for online and offline Australian publications.

His websites—

www.astrology.com.au and
www.face reader.com

attract hundreds of thousands of visitors each month and offer a wide variety of features, helpful information and services.

MESSAGE FROM DADHICHI

Hello and welcome to your 2013 horoscope book!

The key to any successful relationship is communication. This is no secret and relates not only to personal one-on-one romantic relationships, but relationships in general. During 2013, the transit of Jupiter through the sign of Gemini highlights the fact that communication is the foundation of happiness and understanding in relationships. If you've been avoiding talking, sharing your feelings or opening up to the one you love, you can't expect your relationship to go very far, can you?

Effective communication is a form of self-education in which you are open to listening to another's point of view, adapting yourself and at some stage changing your habitual psychological patterns to accommodate the person you love. This can also be translated to business relationships, political interactions and any other relationship in which we empathise and feel the other person's needs.

Many of us are so busy trying to change the world that we forget that a better world starts with our own selves, which is why I am highlighting the fact that communication and self-improvement are the starting point for improving the world at large. By avoiding this, we shift responsibility to someone else and ultimately become the victims of our own lives.

The deeper level of relationships has to do with sexual intimacy. Saturn in the sign of Scorpio points to the fact that the coming 12 months will test us in this area of our lives and we need to be conscious that physical intimacy is really only an extension of our psychological and emotional connectedness to others. It doesn't matter which star sign you are born under, these planets will affect all of us in much the same way. Of course, depending on your Sun sign, the way in which you deal with this will change, but make no mistake about it; communication and intimacy are extremely important keywords for this coming period of time.

Fortunately, Jupiter expands our awareness, so this means we are more likely to be open to the possibilities of being ready, willing and able to meet people halfway and truly identify with where they are at. Once this happens, you will start to feel the benefits of true communication. But clear communication is not just about the words that come out of our mouths. It has more to do with feeling the other person's point of view and doing our best to compassionately understand what they are trying to convey.

This year I have made it a point not to focus too much on bigger-picture predictions but rather to simplify the message by saying that 'charity begins at home'. In reflecting the true traits of Jupiter, we must endeavour to do our best by helping our nearest and dearest, listening to their needs and largely doing what needs to be done on the home front before we look further afield.

Education isn't so much about degrees, diplomas and other intellectual accomplishments as it is about developing wisdom through a sensitive understanding of the experiences that life brings us. If Jupiter is to be of any use to us during 2013, we need to be receptive to the most personal aspects of our lives and express the lessons through loving, intimate relationships.

I look forward to being of service to you and hope that these forecasts for the coming 12 months will be of special value in helping you shape your destiny.

Your astrologer,

Dadhichi Toth
www.astrology.com.au
dadhichi@astrology.com.au

CONTENTS

Aquarius Profile 13
Aquarius Snapshot 14
Aquarius Overview 17
Aquarius Cusps 21
Aquarius Celebrities 24

Aquarius at Large 29
Aquarius Man 30
Aquarius Woman 35
Aquarius Child 39
Aquarius Lover 42
Aquarius Friend 46
Aquarius Enemy 49

Aquarius at Home 51
Home Front 52
Karma, Luck and Meditation 54
Health, Wellbeing and Diet 56
Finance Finesse 58

CONTENTS
CONTINUED

Aquarius at Work **59**

Aquarius Career 60

Aquarius Boss 63

Aquarius Employee 65

Professional Relationships: Best and Worst 67

Aquarius in Love **71**

Romantic Compatibility 72

Horoscope Compatibility for Aquarius 76

Aquarius Partnerships 80

Platonic Relationships: Best and Worst 85

Sexual Relationships: Best and Worst 89

Quiz: Have You Found Your Perfect Match? 94

2013: Yearly Overview **99**

Key Experiences 100

Romance and Friendship 101

Work and Money 105

Health, Beauty and Lifestyle 112

Karma, Spirituality and Emotional Balance 117

CONTENTS
CONTINUED

2013: Monthly and Daily Predictions **119**

January 120

February 126

March 131

April 136

May 142

June 147

July 153

August 159

September 164

October 170

November 176

December 182

2013: Astronumerology **189**

The Power Behind Your Name 190

Your Planetary Ruler 197

Your Planetary Forecast 199

AQUARIUS
PROFILE

UNLESS YOU CHOOSE TO DO GREAT THINGS WITH IT, IT MAKES NO DIFFERENCE HOW MUCH YOU ARE REWARDED, OR HOW MUCH POWER YOU HAVE.

Oprah Winfrey

AQUARIUS SNAPSHOT

Key Life Phrase	I Progress
Zodiac Totem	The Water Bearer
Zodiac Symbol	♒
Zodiac Facts	Eleventh sign of the zodiac; fixed, barren, masculine and dry
Zodiac Element	Air
Key Characteristics	Detached, progressive, humane, intellectual, flamboyant, sympathetic and unpredictable
Compatible Star Signs	Aries, Gemini, Libra and Sagittarius

Mismatched Signs	Pisces, Taurus, Cancer, Leo, Virgo, Scorpio and Capricorn
Ruling Planets	Uranus and Saturn
Love Planets	Mercury and the Sun
Finance Planets	Neptune and Jupiter
Speculation Planet	Mercury
Career Planets	Mars, Pluto and the Moon
Spiritual and Karmic Planets	Venus and Mercury
Friendship Planet	Jupiter
Destiny Planet	Mercury
Famous Aquarians	Jerry Springer, John Travolta, Natalie Imbruglia, Garth Brooks, Nick Nolte, Seth Green, Diane Lane, Oprah Winfrey, Tom Selleck, Gene Hackman, Ellen Degeneres, Phil Collins, Paris Hilton, Charles Darwin, Abraham Lincoln, Jennifer Aniston, Peter Gabriel, Lisa Marie Presley and Justin Timberlake

Lucky Numbers and Significant Years	4, 5, 6, 13, 14, 15, 22, 23, 24, 31, 32, 33, 40, 41, 42, 50, 51, 53, 58, 60, 67, 68, 77, 78, 86, 87 and 88
Lucky Gems	Blue sapphire, amethyst, green emerald, green tourmaline, diamond and lapis lazuli
Lucky Fragrances	Star anise, lavender, rose and pine
Affirmation/ Mantra	I evolve and encompass all humanity
Lucky Days	Wednesday, Friday and Saturday

AQUARIUS OVERVIEW

Born under the sign of Aquarius, the eleventh in the mystical circle of the heavens, you are ruled by the electric and progressive planet Uranus. This makes you forward-thinking and independent in the way you approach most things in life. Actually, you could be termed a born rebel!

Telling you what to do and how to live is a waste of time. From an early age you are broad-minded, and your visionary attitude makes it abundantly clear just how different you are to the general population.

You may be criticised for your rebellious attitude, but you'd rather see yourself as an independent and self-sufficient human being, rather than one of the sheep that follows a tried-and-true path. Boring!

Your energy levels are amazing, and although you want to use this to run your life any way you want, you may not always be able to break free of the limits imposed on you. Some Aquarians learn, mostly through their family, that before you can be master of your own destiny, you have to serve it. If an Aquarian is controlled and dominated by others in the formative years of their life, it will be difficult for them to submit to others in the future.

You have a bubbly personality, thanks to your ruling planet, Uranus. Others are attracted to you because

Aquarian Dreamer

If circumstances prevent you from living life on your own terms, it won't stop you from dreaming about it and aspiring to a time when you can explore your destiny in exactly the way you want.

of your transparent, clear, fun-loving ways. You make a strong impression only when people are able to get beyond the cool exterior that you use to protect your inner self.

You share your zodiac sign with many other inspirational personalities who are involved in social and humanitarian projects. You like to be involved in groups and organisations that can make a difference in society, even in small ways. As your life progresses, your Aquarian nature will inspire

you to make a difference wherever you can. The higher side of Aquarius is attracted to charitable, social and humanitarian works. You have a selflessness that can be used to uplift the world, and this may be your greatest asset in life. You're able to help others in their time of need, and because you are sincere and straightforward in your manner of dealing with others, you are held in high esteem by most who know you.

You are also investigative, curious and mentally active. The Aquarian brain rarely, if ever, stops, and the only downside of this is that you need to learn how to put your brain into neutral so you can sleep at night. This is not easy for an Aquarian, but it is possible.

THE BOLD COMMUNICATOR

Your forté is communication, and your ideas require you to interact boldly with the world around you so you can continue to develop your active personality. There's never a dull moment when an Aquarian is putting forward a bold concept to those who have a far more conventional outlook. You'll be more than happy to challenge their ideas, and will take great pleasure in proving them wrong.

There is never a dull moment with you, Aquarius. Even if you have a fairly stable home or work situation, you like to shake things up now and again, just to keep everyone on their toes.

Because your domestic situation is ruled by the planet Venus, you are very loyal when it comes to your home life and close relationships. The combination of Uranus, Saturn and Venus impact on your home life, which means that you exhibit a flair for design and colour. This will show in the way you furnish your surroundings. It will be far from ordinary, but it will certainly have your unique stamp on it.

You will find it difficult to maintain relationships with those who aren't prepared to evolve or develop in the same way as you. This may cause you to continually re-invent yourself and try to motivate your circle of friends to evolve with you. One could probably say that you are like a chameleon, changing colour as the situation requires. But, at the end of the day, you have to be true to yourself first.

Your inflexibility of opinion sometimes brings you into disagreement with those you regard as near and dear. One of the laws of power suggests that it's okay to act like others, and that it's not always good to openly air your thoughts. Aquarians need to keep some of their radical ideas tucked away until they thoroughly test the waters with the people they're involved with.

AQUARIUS CUSPS

ARE YOU A CUSP BABY?

Being born on the crossover of two star signs means that you have the qualities of both. Sometimes you don't know whether you're Arthur or Martha! Some of my clients can't quite figure out whether they are indeed their own star sign or the one before or after. This is to be expected because being born on the borderline means you take on aspects of both. The following will give you an overview of the subtle effects of these cusp dates and how they affect your personality.

Aquarius–Capricorn Cusp

The signs of Aquarius and Capricorn are diametrically opposed, so if you're born in the cuspal interval during the overlap of these two signs—from the 21st to the 28th January—you take on elements of the preceding sign of Capricorn. This blend of Aquarius and Capricorn energies can create some problems for you. The Aquarian part of your sign will want to progress and move forward, while the Capricorn element will drag you back to being conservative and traditional. This pushing and pulling, so to speak, will probably result in considerable confusion for you.

This tug-of-war will also be evident in the way you relate to people. The Aquarian influence will make you generous and helpful, both locally and worldwide. The Capricorn side will be persistently mindful of the consequences of your generosity. It will be reluctant to give away your worldly goods, whether they are still useful to you or not.

My advice to you, Aquarius, is not to use up too much energy fighting these diametrically opposed personality traits. In fact, just accept the qualities of both star signs—and there are many—and you will still be successful and secure, which is the Capricornian ideal, and capable of progression, to satisfy the Aquarian side of your nature. In this way, you will truly have the best of both worlds.

A DELICATE BALANCE

If you don't have the financial resources to pursue your life the way you want, this cuspal burden will place a lot of strain on you. Finding a delicate balance will be part of life's challenge for you, Aquarius.

Aquarius–Pisces Cusp

The sign following Aquarius is Pisces, so if you happen to be born between the 12th and the 19th of February, you will exhibit the traits of both Aquarius and the sign of the Fish, Pisces.

If you are born during this cuspal period, you may come across as being detached and even insensitive, but you actually care deeply for your fellow man. A very diverse group of friends and associates will be attracted to you and you will live life with a view to exploring every aspect of your relationships, with the ultimate goal of having a more enlightened view of the world and yourself.

A BORN HUMANITARIAN

Pisces is the final sign of the zodiac, and it can karmically represent the last stage of human evolution. Pisceans have a strong emotional and devout quality to their personality. This, combined with the intellectual and spiritual quality of Aquarius, results in an individual with a strong desire to help others.

Be mindful when it comes to your generosity. It is not always wise to give just for the sake of giving, and your Aquarian side should come to the fore to discriminate over who is worthy of your help and who is there to take advantage of you.

Your friends have a hard time keeping up with you as you evolve so rapidly that it makes their head spin. Then there are others who will try to hold you back from your headlong rush to save the world. There's an old saying that you might want to keep in mind: 'Think as you like, but act like others'. This may be necessary if your ways are too idealistic for the people around you.

AQUARIUS CELEBRITIES

FAMOUS MALE: JERRY SPRINGER

What other star sign could Jerry Springer be but an Aquarian! His confrontational, often shocking, talk show typifies the progressive and revolutionary attitude of Aquarian natives.

Jerry was born on the 13th of February, 1944, and began his career in the conservative field of law. Before this, he earned his Bachelor of Arts degree in political science he was extremely dedicated to upholding the freedom of the American Constitution. Freedom is one of the key words of the Aquarian star sign, and this again demonstrates Jerry Springer's Aquarian personality. This personality trait is so strong that Jerry has continued to be an advocate of constitutional change and has also shown a tremendous interest in political activism over the years.

Aquarius is considered a sign of man, and is deeply connected to humanitarian ideals and the continual development and improvement of political and social laws. Being a true Aquarian, we see why Jerry Springer has done his best to make these political objectives his life mission.

Some of the Aquarian character traits of wilfulness, intellectual aggressiveness and unexpected or zany behaviour are also reflected in the way he produces his television shows. We see the bizarre and the ridiculous combined in the talkback segment at the end of each show. It's obvious that Jerry Springer injects his Aquarian humour where he can. He has even appeared in several comedies, including *Austin Powers 2: The Spy Who Shagged Me* (1999).

Aquarius is an earth sign and concerned with intellectual issues, which is probably why Jerry helped establish an educational scholarship to fund the Kellman School in Chicago. This fund helps the inner-city youth of Chicago develop their skills. He is also actively involved in the Audrey Hepburn Hollywood for Children Fund and often attends telethons to assist medical causes. As a humanitarian sign, it is clear that the Aquarian individual takes to charitable work like a fish to water!

FAMOUS FEMALE: ELLEN DeGENERES

Ellen DeGeneres was born on the 26th of January 1958, and this makes her an Aquarian born on the cusp of Capricorn.

Cleverness and intellectual wit are some of the highlights of the Aquarius personality, and Ellen displays a great deal of these characteristics in her award-winning talk show, which has become a hit with millions of people around the world.

Along with great ratings, her talk show has won unparalleled accolades from the entertainment industry, winning no less than 15 Emmy Awards in its first three seasons on the air. It also became the first talk show in television history to win the Emmy Award for Outstanding Talk Show throughout its initial three seasons.Although Ellen studied communication at a major university—which shouldn't surprise us as the Aquarian native is always hungry for knowledge—she dropped out after one semester and decided to try stand-up comedy.

Ellen has had tremendous success as a comedian, and even as early as 1980 she was named the funniest person in America. Of course, this led to bigger and better things, and in 1986 she made her debut on *The Johnny Carson Show*. In 1994 she starred in the popular sitcom, *Ellen*, which ran until 1998, and the rest, as they say, is history.

In 1997 she came out of the closet and declared her homosexuality. She has since been open about her sexual preferences, which Aquarians are known to do, as well as using it to progress humanity and its gay and lesbian minority groups.

AQUARIUS
AT LARGE

THE MORE SAND THAT HAS ESCAPED FROM THE HOURGLASS OF OUR LIFE, THE CLEARER WE SHOULD SEE THROUGH IT.

Jean Paul

AQUARIUS MAN

♂

AQUARIUS MAN: SNAPSHOT

Pioneering

Open-minded

Unruly

Opinionated

Idealistic

Intuitive

Many books on astrology describe the Aquarian male as aloof, cool, detached and somewhat uninvolved in the circumstances around them. But don't be fooled. Underneath that cool exterior is a passionate, determined individual working with great commitment to achieve larger-than-life goals.

The appearance of the Aquarius male is generally, but not always, tall, heavy-boned and well built. The Aquarian male is instantly noticed as he has a commanding way about him and the way he approaches life.

As an Aquarian male, your humour probably ranges from bizarre to dry cynicism, which is due to your perceptiveness and the ability to see possibilities others may have missed. Unfortunately, many conventional people don't know what to make of you, but this doesn't trouble you in the least.

AN INDEPENDENT SPIRIT

You are an independent character with a dislike for authority, especially in the traditional sense. You are a rebel at heart and like to fight against all forms of control that you see as limiting progress, growth and human evolution.

Change and non-conformity are a distinct part of your character, and when dealing with others and getting involved in a relationship, you will quickly find out whether they're going to accept you or not. Either way, there's not much that's going to change your point of view and the path you have chosen.

Aspects of your personality may shock others, and in your own perverse way you enjoy this trait. You may even be faced with challenges in life where the only way to rebuild a situation is to totally demolish it and start again. This is not an idea that will be accepted by everyone, but it won't stop you doing it if you have the power and control to do so.

However, you need to learn to be respectful of people's opinions as well as your own. You are generally fair in your views and hate to see any form of injustice, which is why you are drawn to humanitarian pursuits, particularly where people are taking advantage of those less fortunate.

You love change and will often drop what you are doing for an exciting adventure or new challenge. This can leave people puzzled, but you dread the thought of missing an opportunity and feel that you can always pick up where you left off.

Exploring the world, society and different philosophical views will always be part of your personality. You're creative by nature, so you don't do very well in roles where physical or mental mobility is limited. You need scope, self-sufficiency, creativity and, above all, mutual respect from those you live and work with. These things are of utmost importance to you.

You have a diverse range of interests, be they intellectual, physical or practical. You fear being at a loss for something to do. But this is not likely given the way you live your life, Aquarius. You keep boredom at bay by always seeking out new things and places.

Sport appeals to you, as well as travelling and exploring different cultures, religions and philosophies. You are a teacher of sorts and can often see hidden meaning in things that escape those who are less evolved in the world.

When you were a small child, you probably asked 'why' a lot, even when you knew you should be seen and not heard. Going against the 'norm' is second nature to you, and you must have driven your parents to distraction with your constant questioning. You have a thirst for knowledge and spend your life trying to find answers and solutions to questions that others may not even think to ask.

You have wonderful leadership qualities and offer tremendous inspiration to others, but you don't easily submit to those who are in a position of control. Accepting rules and regulations is not one of your strong points. Until you're in a position where you can bend the rules to suit your needs, you may have to go along with them.

You have strong willpower and become impatient with anyone who's not quick to grasp your ideas. Learning patience, and accepting others for who they are, will be one of the biggest challenges in your life. Try to be respectful of other people's opinions as well.

You are fast, energetic and have a great deal of self-confidence. You are fair and balanced in your views and partake of the Libran air sign's theme of justice. You hate to see any form of injustice, which is why you're drawn to humanitarian pursuits.

You can have a ferocious temper, particularly in matters of the heart, romance and marriage. This could prove to be your undoing, and you must learn to bring balance into your emotional life. If you can do this, you will be a much happier and more fulfilled individual.

AQUARIUS WOMAN

♀

AQUARIUS WOMAN: SNAPSHOT

Radical

Original

Charitable

Creative

Nervous

The Aquarian woman likes to see herself as free and unconventional. However, because Aquarius is a male sign, this means that women born under this forward-thinking sign have a masculine quality about them.

Even before women's liberation, the Aquarian woman was attempting to live her life differently. You are always a step ahead of the pack and dislike any form of injustice, which is why you'll be the one to make a stand for women in all classes of society.

You are not one to follow traditional ways of life and find it very easy to express yourself. Your views on life, love and social affairs will fascinate others and you are constantly busy with organisations where you put all of these talents to good use.

You like watching people as you learn a lot from others. Individuals from different walks of life will captivate you. Culture and foreign affairs will also arouse your curiosity. It may even lead you to travel far and wide, but if circumstances prevent you from actually travelling, then you will seek out unusual cultures in your local area.

THE ETERNAL STUDENT

With your keen intellect, you will have a diverse range of hobbies and activities. You have a thirst for knowledge and this makes you an eternal student. You will never finish learning, no matter what your age.

Men generally feel intimidated by women who possess as much power as you, Aquarius. Make sure that the mate you choose stands head and shoulders above the rest, and not just in a physical way. You'll maintain a group consciousness until you meet the right person—and you will be quite selective during the process. You have to be sure that your partner has a similar level of understanding and social conscience. Until you find that special someone, you may appear to be aloof, unapproachable and even fickle. This is just a façade and has nothing to do with what motivates you, Aquarius.

Your friends and those who know you well, particularly family members, are likely to refer to you as hypersensitive. You do need to be careful as there are moments when you take others' statements too personally. In any case, your heart is in the right place and your motives are pure.

Routine and the general humdrum aspects of life are not on your agenda. You are unpredictable in the way you do things, so there doesn't seem to be any rhyme or reason to your schedule. You may do this for shock value because you like to unsettle others and push them beyond their comfort zone. This works well for you most of the time, but you should keep in mind that your offbeat tactics may have long-term consequences in our traditional society. This is never truer than in the professional field.

You spend a lot of time and energy bringing harmony to your environment, and this can work in your favour in the workplace. You can be the perfect mediator in troubled relationships, and with your natural talent you are able to stand back and impartially find a solution to their problems.

There are moments when the Aquarian woman feels a little lonely and unsupported. The truth is that you usually give more than what you receive. There is an imbalance in this equation, which will result in some deep-seated sorrow. You need to rectify this by asking for what you want rather than expecting people to guess. Speak out, Aquarius.

You have a quirky sense of humour, quick wit and possess excellent intuition. This psychic ability may not always be obvious to others as you tend to operate differently to your colleagues. Your knack for dressing uniquely will also set you apart from others. However, if the mood takes you, you have the ability to adapt to convention as well.

AQUARIUS CHILD

The Aquarian child has, first and foremost, a mind of their own. On this issue there are no half-measures for parents, and being able to discover a fair way of disciplining them will be a challenge. Yes, they are wilful, challenging and at times inflexible, but try to remember that you are dealing with an old soul who can see through your adult strategies.

Your Aquarian child will challenge you on almost every level. When it comes to discipline or getting them to follow a guideline or schedule, your instructions need to be clear and precise. They will challenge you, but you need to stand firm as you are preparing them for the world at large.

When they are older and become more acquainted with the realities of life, they will find that there are certain parameters within which they must abide. Without an earlier grounding, they will be very unhappy individuals.

They have brilliant intellectual abilities and first-rate observation skills. Combine this with second-to-none problem-solving abilities, and you have quite a challenge on your hands.

The Aquarian child likes to play, seeking out the most unusual places and games. To keep their active mind stimulated will take a lot of imagination, particularly if you don't want them to dismantle the electric appliances in the house to see how they work. The ruling planet of Aquarius is Uranus, and its symbol is the aerial and electricity, so it's no wonder they are fascinated by anything electrical.

Beware of Danger

Aquarian children love risky adventures, which is why you'll have to constantly monitor their activities. As they grow older, this penchant for tempting fate will become more evident. Keep them mentally active and steer them towards play that is creative and flexible, making sure that the element of danger is reduced as much as possible.

The first word they will probably utter is 'why?', so you had better be on your toes if you want to stay one jump ahead of your curious Aquarian. They love to talk and find out as much as they can on subjects that interest them. Never stifle this tendency; it is their lifeblood and will stay with them all their life.

Aquarian children, like their brother sign, Gemini, require a peaceful environment to calm their nerves and provide a safe haven in which to develop. Give them room to breathe, and make sure that they do more sport than the average child so they can direct their energies into strategic activities. This will improve their health and relax their minds. It will also short-circuit their argumentative streak.

When choosing the best method of education for your Aquarian child, you will need to look outside the square of conventional schooling. They just won't fit in. Traditional methods will stifle their creativity, and rules and regulations are just too much for them to handle.

The wisdom of Aquarius is inherent in them, so you should never underestimate the maturity that is part and parcel of their character. If you respect this trait, you'll easily bring out their better side. Tact and diplomacy will also go a long way when there is a difference of opinion. If they are forced in any way, they will dig in their heels in and nobody will win.

AQUARIUS LOVER

The Aquarian is a unique and original character, and so too are the relationships they are destined to have. Although they are unconventional, there is still room in their life for traditional relationships.

If you could write out a 'wish list' for your perfect partner, Aquarius, it is unlikely that anyone would pass the test. It would contain some off-the-wall traits, but at least you are honest about what you want. You prefer your relationships to be a bit different, but once you meet the person of your choice, you are loyal and loving.

Your feelings about romance are strong, and the way you express them will require a partner who can sensitively understand where you're coming from. They'll have to give you sufficient room to express your opinions and develop in a way that is comfortable for you.

However, if you find yourself in a situation in which the other party tries to exert control over any aspect of your life, this will be a great blow to the relationship. The way you choose to live your life needs the support of the other person. If they don't give it, then you will waste no time in cutting yourself free. Many Aquarians prefer to remain single for as long as possible because freedom is an essential part of their lifestyle. You could even say that it is as essential as breathing.

The way you show your love may be a little disconcerting for those brought up in a traditional environment, so test the waters before shocking people with your antics. You have no problem asking for your needs to be met, no matter what those needs may be. You are honest, even blunt at times, and there will be no ambiguity in what you are saying.

Your independence is non-negotiable in romantic relationships, even though you're a loyal and trusted friend or lover. This will be the critical foundation of any relationship you enter into. If you are fortunate enough to meet someone who can respect this need, then it will make life much easier and enhance your love for that person.

COMMITTED AQUARIUS

Aquarians have a humanitarian ideal, and this progressive side of their nature provides the foundation for a commitment that can be, and usually is, rock solid.

There's a strong social element to the sign of Aquarius, and your partner will need to accept this. Parties, groups, clubs and organisations that are connected with spiritual or social issues, but that also offer a socially entertaining backdrop, are all necessary for your mental and emotional wellbeing. If your partner is prepared to join in and support you in these endeavours, all will be well. However, if your partner is insular and unaware of the world's needs, then you won't stick around.

Variety is the spice of life for you. This doesn't mean that you are not loyal, but you need plenty of variety in life from which to draw your life experiences. You have a large circle of friends and like to relate to each one in your own special way. You love sharing and caring, but always against a backdrop of your own independence.

There are extreme Aquarians who want to explore inter-personal relationships that are sometimes considered out of bounds or taboo. In your pursuit of anything new, however, you're really still seeking the truth through your own experience of life, and you must be free to do so on your own terms.

When it comes to marriage, the sign of Leo and the Sun dominate this area of your life. It's a well-known fact that the sign of Leo is one of the most loyal and trusted signs of the zodiac. It shows, too, that you're attracted to people who have strong egos and radiate dramatic flair in the way they deal with the world. You need someone who is your equal and who demonstrates loyalty even though you may want the freedom to enjoy many relationships. And when I say this, I don't necessarily mean sexual relationships.

When the question of marriage arises, you must have a partner who is your equal but who will allow you to have the freedom to explore your intellectual and social interests. This is such an important part of your nature that it is almost non-negotiable, and your partner will need to know this if the relationship is to survive.

AQUARIUS FRIEND

As you are born under the eleventh sign of the zodiac, which is the zone of friendship and social activity, you have a natural attraction to humanitarianism. Being a friend is second nature to you, and you will extend the hand of friendship to many who cross your path.

Your effervescent personality is a result of your ruling planet, Uranus. You radiate a very high vibration that acts as a natural attractant. People are usually deeply impressed by you and want to be your friend because you tend to be impartial in the way you treat others. It doesn't matter whether they wear silk or sackcloth; they will be treated equally.

You have a generous nature and like the idea of helping others. Early in your life you may be attracted to charities or social work, and you also go the extra mile to lift others out of their problems. However, you need to be mindful of giving advice when it is not asked for. It can put people offside, particularly when they don't like what you have to say.

Although you like to maintain control over your feelings, letting down your guard with people you trust can be beneficial for you. It will make you seem more human and will help others relate to you better.

A STRAIGHT-SHOOTER

You listen patiently and take on board what others say, even if it differs from your viewpoint. Your friends can always rely on the fact that you will give an honest opinion. Some may say that you are a bit too straightforward, but that is the way you are. Take it or leave it—it's their choice.

For the most part, your friendships will be based on intellectual pursuits. As an air sign, you need to have a direct connection with the minds of others. It's through this mental connection that you are able to relate to the emotional aspects of the friendship. You get bored easily and want friends to have some level of experience that matches yours. You like history, philosophy, psychology and other interesting scientific or technological discussions. For someone to be a true friend, they must have the ability to share ideas at this intellectual level.

You're loyal and bighearted and your loved ones know they can rely on you. That's because you don't just talk about your philosophy, you live it. Sincerity and straightforwardness are some of your greatest assets, and this is always evident in the advice you give. It may not be typical, but it will always be practical. When it comes to reciprocation from your friends, you expect loyalty and support in your endeavours. Free-thinking individuals will probably make up the majority of your social circle as each of you will understand where the other is coming from.

You are spontaneous and others will never be bored by your company. You like to challenge the status quo, which is your way of improving yourself and helping others as well.

AQUARIUS ENEMY

There is a difference between sticking to your guns and obstinately refusing to budge. Your opinions can at times be inflexible, and, although you do have a quick wit and a brilliant ability to see beyond the 'norm', you must learn to accept that there are other viewpoints.

If you want to keep your friends, be mindful of how your express your opinions. Being uncompromising will only turn those friends into enemies. Be aware of how you come across when trying to win a point.

You can be rebellious, and your desire to innovate and shock may put others at odds with you. There's no problem exploring life and changing things, as long as you don't do it in a way that is abrupt and disrespectful.

You can be explosive due to the rulership of Uranus over your sign. If you are pushed too far, it may force you to exhibit this side of your nature. For many who haven't witnessed it previously, it may come as a bit of a shock. Try to exercise more balance in your life and use your wonderful powers of transformation in a way that doesn't unsettle others.

AQUARIUS
AT HOME

GOOD JUDGMENT COMES FROM EXPERIENCE, AND OFTEN EXPERIENCE COMES FROM BAD JUDGMENT.

Rita Mae Brown

HOME FRONT

As an air sign, Aquarians love space and room to breathe. You need room to express your rather unusual personality, and you are more than likely to live in a contemporary home that is decorated with lots of bits and pieces you have lovingly collected.

You like to mix and match colours in your home much like the way you dress. Safe and conservative are two words you don't include when making decisions about your lifestyle or home furnishings, just as the classic suit is not something you would wear to work.

Those who are more traditional may find your home a bit confronting. But its many styles and colours come together and match you perfectly. You tend to stay away from the modern and minimalist as you find that they don't have any warmth or feeling.

When choosing your furniture, think calm and peaceful, because your home is where you will be at the end of the day. Partying and socialising is fine, but there is nothing that soothes the soul like a home that reflects your tastes and represents what you have done and where you have been in your life.

Your collection of bits and pieces from your adventures will have pride of place, and it doesn't matter whether anyone likes your choices or not. You like comfort, but are not keen on fussy, overstuffed couches with cushions arranged neatly along the back.

You are more of a leader than a follower, which is why books on the latest gadgets, styles or fabrics will be missing from your coffee table. It is more likely that you will have books on Feng Shui as you want to get the elements of your home just right. As you are an air sign, your home will have a layout that keeps the flow and movement of air in mind. Music, wind chimes, candles and incense can create the right mood when you are home alone or sharing your space with friends. With Uranus as your ruling planet, your style is eclectic and electric. The colours that will enhance this mood are iridescent blues and green, multi-coloured rainbows and chequered or zigzagged colours that reflect what an Aquarian is all about.

To create a glow and reflect light, use glass or mirrors that will bounce the light back into the room and give a feeling of space. Lamps and candles can also provide the right ambience when the sun goes down. Electronics will also be important as they reflect the Aquarian love of technological advancement, and you could include computers or surround sound systems in your décor to complete the mood you want to create.

KARMA, LUCK AND MEDITATION

Your life phrase is 'I progress', which means that you push the boundaries wherever you go. This helps you develop your spiritual and psychic abilities. You intuitively know that you will never develop your full potential if you stay with the tried and true. This is what gives many Aquarians their strong spiritual nature.

LIVING BY THEIR OWN RULES

Aquarians generally find their own way through life, usually living by their own rules and relying on experience to work out the mysteries they are presented with daily.

Your ruling planet of past karma and good fortune is Venus, and its star sign is Libra. This is an air sign and a very social one as well. This means that you are quite lucky in relation to others and often use your charm and personality to win the hearts of many. You are also endowed with intuitive energy and this helps steer you in the right direction spiritually. However, you don't go along with a religion or philosophy without thoroughly testing it and seeing whether or not it suits you.

Your nervous system can be a little compromised at times. To soothe your nerves, you are advised to meditate on Wednesday, Friday and Saturday. This will help you expand your awareness, which will lead to health and personal fulfilment. These days are also lucky for your spiritual and personal development. If you can spend a little time each day clearing your thoughts and becoming more aware of your inner self, you will accelerate your spiritual development.

Lucky Days

Your luckiest days are Wednesday, Friday and Saturday.

Lucky Numbers

Lucky numbers for Aquarius include the following. You may wish to experiment with these in lotteries and other games of chance:

5, 14, 23, 32, 41, 50

6, 15, 24, 33, 42, 51

8, 17, 26, 35, 44, 53

Destiny Years

Your most important years are: 4, 5, 6, 13, 14, 15, 22, 23, 24, 31, 32, 33, 40, 41, 42, 50, 51, 53, 58, 60, 67, 68, 77, 78, 86, 87 and 88.

HEALTH, WELLBEING AND DIET

Aquarius is an air sign and this influences the thinking processes and nervous system. These areas need careful consideration if you're to maintain optimum health and vitality. You need to keep a regular regime of work, play, sleep and dietary habits, and by doing this you will be able to maintain good health and enjoy a long life.

Aquarius rules the lower part of the body, particularly your shins and ankles. Proper exercise is needed to strengthen these areas, increase flexibility and maintain good circulation. Hatha yoga will perfectly meet all of the above criteria. Aquarians are known for their circulation problems, especially as they age.

You have an active mind and an intense desire to do a lot of work. This will undermine your vitality if you don't have a balanced diet, and you could become prone to vitamin deficiencies in the B, C and K groups. These are vitamins that can rebuild your nerve and skin tissue and make your bones much denser. This will also help you to overcome such things as osteoporosis in later life.

You might like to take a supplement of these vitamins to give you the building blocks of health and vitality. Other foods such as soybean products, bean sprouts, egg, wheat germ and white meats are all natural sources of these vitamins. Because of your progressive thinking, a macrobiotic diet is something you could try, and quite likely with excellent results.

Try including vegetables such as broccoli, lettuce, spinach, potatoes (in moderation), mandarins, mangoes and low-fat cheese to increase your intake of essential vitamins and minerals. Additionally, by including bean sprouts such as mung and alfalfa, and green seafood like kelp, you'll start to really enjoy wonderful health. Your ruling planet Uranus is an erratic planet and you should avoid eating when excessively excited as this could lead to intestinal upsets. Learning to relax will also have a tonic effect on your whole body.

FINANCE FINESSE

You are such a spontaneous individual, Aquarius, that money slips through your fingers and you are surprised when it has all gone. You need to monitor what you buy, but more importantly, you need to work out why you are buying the things that use up so much of your money. Is it 'want' or 'need'?

You want to change the world with your progressive ideas, but you can be somewhat wilful when it comes to spending money. You will save money for something special, but then spend it on an object that has caught your eye. Another thing that will derail your savings plan is your love of humanitarian pursuits and your selflessness when it comes to helping those less fortunate.

The sign of Pisces, with its rulers Jupiter and Venus, regulates the way you earn money. Although money is not your main reason for working, you like to measure your success through bank deposits and keeping your balance in the black.

Sagittarius and Jupiter rule your zone of profitability, which means that you can earn good money from whatever work you choose. You are also honest and above board with your dealings, and you expect nothing less from those you work with.

AQUARIUS
AT WORK

START BY DOING WHAT'S NECESSARY, THEN DO WHAT'S POSSIBLE, AND SUDDENLY YOU ARE DOING THE IMPOSSIBLE.

St Francis of Assisi

AQUARIUS CAREER

IDEAL PROFESSIONS

Consultant

Entrepreneur

Inventor

Scientist

Astrologer and/or psychic

Radio, television or media presenter

Archaeologist

Medical worker or researcher

Electronics engineer

IT or communications specialist

Journalist

Coming up with ideas is second nature to you, Aquarius, and you can communicate this quite well to the people you work with. You are a team player and like to engage with others to improve the quality of the work being done as well as the interpersonal relationships of your colleagues.

You need a career that engages your mind, and some suitable roles would be entrepreneur, inventor, scientist, astrologer, psychic, researcher, electronics engineer or communications consultant. However, you need to have variety and do things that will generally uplift people. Humanitarian work is what you do best, which is why social work would also appeal. You like new causes as well and are a fan of environmental and cultural change for the betterment of the human race.

CITIZEN OF THE WORLD

You have an adaptable mind and are able to work almost anywhere in the world, which appeals to your love of travel and freedom. You love to explore, and with your curious mind you will feel at home anywhere on this planet.

You have a broad knowledge base, and although you care about the world you live in, you also need to have some financial success. This can be achieved by using technology to both further your ambitions and create projects that can help those in developing countries, thus satisfying your humanitarian instincts.

A day filled with boring repetitive tasks is your idea of a living hell, and if you find yourself in this situation, learn to delegate—rapidly. It is not that these tasks are too mundane for you; it is just that they stifle your creativity and well-developed intellectual mind.

You are sensitive about your work. You appear cool and calm on the outside, but you identify so closely with your work that it can affect you in ways that are unknown to others. You need to communicate your feelings; don't let them get bottled up and cause you stress. And learn to relax in the workplace, or you might be seen as demanding and manipulative.

AQUARIUS BOSS

If you are working for an Aquarian boss, you can rest assured that they don't play favourites. They will make decisions solely based on what is best for the business, and personalities will not come into the equation.

You can be absolutely confident that your Aquarian boss will be fair, and although they can sometimes be unpredictable, they will have the welfare of their employees at heart.

If you make a mistake, it would be in your best interests to own up. Trying to fool your Aquarian boss would be an extremely bad idea as it just won't work. An Aquarian boss is usually quite forgiving if you are honest with them, and they are more likely to help you improve yourself rather than show you the door.

Although they may sometimes appear distracted, they are highly intuitive and know exactly what is going on at any given minute. They will help you develop you skills and encourage you to learn new ones.

If you come up with a great idea, they will probably have thought of it first. Aquarians are very analytical and will work with you to refine your ideas. It is for this reason that you will be glad you have this particular boss on your side. They will look for qualities in you that will be beneficial to the business as a whole and help you develop those qualities with further training or moving you to an area that enhances your skill base.

They respect individuality in their employees, and, as long as you can work within the general policies of the company, the relationship with your Aquarian boss should be quite satisfactory and fulfilling. By the time you leave the company, if you ever do, of course, your skills will have improved immeasurably.

The Aquarian boss knows how to make a team work well together. They want good dynamics in the workplace and are not happy about individual egos taking pride of place. If you happen to be a one-man-band and don't care whose toes you tread on while you climb the ladder of success, an Aquarian boss could bring you down to earth with a bump.

AQUARIUS EMPLOYEE

At first glance, an Aquarian employee may look as though their brain is off doing something else—and this may well be the case. They could come across as a bit distant or even disconnected from what is going on around them, but this is just their style.

An Aquarian needs to work out exactly where they fit into the scheme of things, so it would be wise for an employer to sit back and not interfere too much at this stage. As an air sign, your Aquarian employee uses their rationality to understand not only the job, but also where they fit in with the rest of the team, the company and even the industry. Once they have gathered this information, they can put the last piece of the puzzle in place—themselves.

ALWAYS COOL-HEADED

If an Aquarian employee is under pressure, you will find that they are quite cool and can manage the situation better than most. They have great analytical skills and are able to work things out much faster than most of their colleagues. A wise boss should use this ability when things are in crisis mode.

Aquarians can come up with brilliant ideas that may seem a little 'out there', but they have usually thought about them at length before putting them out there. They can also come across as a bit weird at times, sometimes engaging in rather bizarre behaviour, but these odd and interesting rituals make them feel and function better in the workplace. Don't read too much into it; for the most part, it will be to the advantage of the boss and the company.

Your Aquarian employee is honest, trustworthy and conscientious. They have a code of conduct that they strictly adhere to and will not let you down. They like to earn a fair day's pay, but you will be more than compensated by some of the ideas they come up with to save time or money for the company.

A wise boss will give them time to explain their somewhat radical concepts and think about their ideas before they are dismissed as impractical or just too weird. Remember, they may take their idea to someone further up the food chain, and you may find yourself working for your Aquarian employee.

PROFESSIONAL RELATIONSHIPS: BEST AND WORST

BEST PAIRING: AQUARIUS AND SAGITTARIUS

Sagittarius is the eleventh sign to Aquarius, and some astrologers believe that this is not a good match for business relationships. However, I disagree because a fire sign is actually fuelled by air and can create a lot of creative energy in some situations, including a business relationship.

Sagittarius is somewhat unstructured when it comes to commerce, and Aquarius doesn't exactly fit the pattern of 'normal' either. The finer details of a business plan need to be undertaken by someone, so this is an area that will have to be worked on. Is this a recipe for failure? Not necessarily.

Sagittarians are optimistic, and when motivated they are ready to push forward with their Aquarian partner. You will stimulate and inspire your Sagittarian partner to direct their considerable energies in a way that can be productive and profitable for you both. They are explorers at heart and will happily look around marketplaces or bazaars to find items that are quirky, interesting or just novel.

Neither of you are greatly concerned with money, but you are both intelligent, focused and can see the bigger picture. You have a broader view of life and humanity and may want to go into partnership in a project that helps other who are less fortunate and unable to help themselves. This will help Sagittarius stimulate the compassionate and spiritual side of their character, while Aquarius will live out this ideal.

You both love travelling and exploring cultures and foreign places that are off the beaten track. These similarities can be put to good use if you decide to ethically source unique products from people in other countries. This will not only improve their standard of living but also help stop the exploitation of people in developing countries.

Even if you have a sales or marketing background, you can leave the display and showcasing to your Sagittarian partner. It is well within their capabilities to make the goods desirable to your client base and increase sales and profitability.

You are both good at earning money, but keeping it could be another story. You may have to employ a third person to take care of the finances if you hope to have a business that is profitable. Both of you tend to do things on a whim, and that also includes spending your hard-earned dollars.

WORST PAIRING: AQUARIUS AND TAURUS

Taurus's approach to economising could stifle you, Aquarius. They are so concerned with security that the purse strings will be hard to access. Taureans resist change and like things to be orderly and secure. You, on the other hand, want the freedom to explore your imagination and ideas and come up with the money to make it all happen. You certainly don't want anything to interfere with your love of freedom and letting your wonderful mind roam where it will.

Money is secondary to your need to help the world and produce something that will be important to others, no matter how large or small. And you want to put your own stamp on what you produce.

While all this creativity is going on, your Taurean friend will be so concerned with issues of security, frugality and economising that they won't be able find the money for the project you wish to bring to fruition. This will cause you endless frustration and exasperation.

Although Taurus must be given credit for keeping the business financially in the black, you'll realise that this business match is not going to be easy. Constant head-on confrontations about money and how to spend it will dry up your creativity very quickly.

Taureans prefer the tried and true; they resist change more than any other star sign. It makes them incredibly nervous, and with your avant garde approach and fearlessness, this is not a relationship that will bring much joy to either of you.

It will be a constant battle of wills, and Taurus will not be comfortable with any changes. They will resent the fact that you are in charge and will not see your forward and expansive thinking as an asset, but as another way to spend money. A business meeting with them will be guaranteed to leave you drained, frustrated and wondering why you bothered in the first place. If you don't have an iron-clad contract, Aquarius, I would advise you take your share of the business and team up with someone who will encourage you to achieve your dreams.

AQUARIUS
IN LOVE

WE ARE ALL A LITTLE WEIRD
AND LIFE'S A LITTLE WEIRD, AND
WHEN WE FIND SOMEONE WHOSE
WEIRDNESS IS COMPATIBLE WITH
OURS, WE JOIN UP WITH THEM AND
FALL IN MUTUAL WEIRDNESS
AND CALL IT LOVE.

Dr Seuss

ROMANTIC COMPATIBILITY

How compatible are you with your current partner, lover or friend? Did you know that astrology can reveal a whole new level of understanding between people simply by looking at their star sign and that of their partner? In this chapter I'd like to share with you some special insights that will help you better appreciate the strengths and challenges using Sun sign compatibility.

The Sun reflects your drive, willpower and personality. The essential qualities of two star signs blend like two pure colours producing an entirely new colour. Relationships, similarly, produce their own emotional colours when two people interact. The following is a general guide to your romantic prospects with others and how by knowing the astrological 'colour' of each other, the art of love can help you create a masterpiece.

When reading the following I ask you to remember that no two star signs are ever *totally* incompatible. With effort and compromise, even the most 'difficult' astrological matches can work. Don't close your mind to the full range of life's possibilities! Learning about each other and ourselves is the most important facet of astrology.

Each star sign combination is followed by the elements of those star signs and the result of their combining: for instance, Aries is a fire sign and Aquarius is an air sign and this combination produces a lot of 'hot air'. Air feeds fire and fire warms air. In fact, fire requires air. However, not all air and fire combinations work. I have included information about the different birth periods within each star sign and this will throw even more light on your prospects for a fulfilling love life with any star sign you choose.

Good luck in your search for love, and may the stars shine upon you in 2013!

STAR SIGN COMPATIBILITY FOR LOVE AND FRIENDSHIP (PERCENTAGES)

	Aries	Taurus	Gemini	Cancer	Leo	Virgo	Libra	Scorpio	Sagittarius	Capricorn	Aquarius	Pisces
Aries	60	65	65	65	90	45	70	80	90	50	55	65
Taurus	60	70	70	80	70	90	75	85	50	95	80	85
Gemini	70	70	75	60	80	75	90	60	75	50	90	50
Cancer	65	80	60	75	70	75	60	95	55	45	70	90
Leo	90	70	80	70	85	75	65	75	95	45	70	75
Virgo	45	90	75	75	75	70	80	85	70	95	50	70
Libra	70	75	90	60	65	80	80	85	80	85	95	50
Scorpio	80	85	60	95	75	85	85	90	80	65	60	95
Sagittarius	90	50	75	55	95	70	80	85	85	55	60	75
Capricorn	50	95	50	45	45	95	85	65	55	85	70	85
Aquarius	55	80	90	70	70	50	95	60	60	70	80	55
Pisces	65	85	50	90	75	70	50	95	75	85	55	80

In the compatibility table above please note that some compatibilities have seemingly contradictory ratings. Why, you ask? Well, remember that no two people experience the relationship in exactly the same way. For one person a relationship may be more advantageous, more supportive than for the other. Sometimes one gains more than the other partner and therefore the compatibility rating will be higher for them.

HOROSCOPE COMPATIBILITY FOR AQUARIUS

Aquarius with		Romance/Sexual
Aries		An exciting relationship, even though you need to sort out where you are going as a couple
Taurus		A lot of patience and perseverance is needed here
Gemini		The bedroom will definitely be the playroom
Cancer		Your bedroom antics may scare Cancer away
Leo		Leo will really light your fire

Friendship		Professional	
✔	You can be yourself with Aries	✘	There could be a lot of differences of opinion; it may get explosive
✘	You have friendly planets, but very different views	✘	Taurus will be manage the money in this match, but you may not like it
✔	A great friendship based on intellect	✔	You could both build a good business
✘	Cancer is a bit too sensitive to your comments	✘	Cancer is trustworthy, but not imaginative enough for you
✔	Boredom is not on this agenda	✔	Challenging, but you will have a great partnership

Aquarius with		Romance/Sexual
Virgo		Don't even go here; they will drive you mad
Libra		You each know what the other wants and will give it
Scorpio		Their sexual intensity will appeal to you
Sagittarius		Fire and air can be explosive
Capricorn		Basic differences; you are worlds apart
Aquarius		Lots of loving, but it can be a bit erratic
Pisces		Pisces is sensitive to you, but will they be able to fulfil you?

	Friendship		Professional
✘	Virgo is far too critical for you; leave this one alone	✘	If you want a good accountant, get a Virgo
✔	Your circle of friends will grow together and social life really buzzes	✔	You are the brains and Libra is good with the sales pitch
✔	You can get down to the nitty-gritty with your Scorpio friend	✔	You can always rely on Scorpio to give solid and loyal support
✔	There is nothing dull and boring about this friendship	✔	Work out the boundaries and responsibilities, and then go for it!
✘	You are dissimilar on so many levels	✔	You could have financial gains if you can live with their traditional approach
✔	A good friendship with much in common	✔	It might work, but you need to set clear guidelines
✘	You may not always gel, but you respect their spirituality	✘	Don't even consider a business deal with Pisces

AQUARIUS PARTNERSHIPS

Aquarius + Aries

You have a strong sense of self and Aries has a powerful ego, so you can expect the odd clash or two. Your intellectual mind and interest in social and humanitarian issues may spark a certain amount of inquisitiveness in Aries. You could bring out each other's best qualities in a relationship.

Aquarius + Taurus

Taurus is traditional, realistic and down-to-earth about most issues in life. You, on the other hand, have a forward-thinking and idealistic view of the world. As long as you have finished sowing your wild oats, a relationship could have a chance, and may even be long term.

Aquarius + Gemini

This is probably a safe bet. There is a positive and strong link between your star signs. You're a rebel at heart and that is exactly what attracts Gemini. You both love variety, excitement and intellectual fulfilment. With your ruling planet, Uranus, you bring energy to any romantic endeavour.

Aquarius + Cancer

Cancer will be wasting their time trying to pull you into line, Aquarius. They may try to impose some stable routine on you, but your freedom-loving ways will have you heading for the hills. Cancer will be the one to compromise in this relationship.

Aquarius + Leo

Leo is your opposite sign, which creates an attraction. Leo recognises your intellectual appetite for life. As you are impulsive and emotional in your responses, so too is Leo, and you may find yourselves married before you have thought too much about it.

Aquarius + Virgo

If you want a challenge, Aquarius, then find yourself a Virgo. You are a big-picture person, whereas Virgo is concerned with the nit-picky details. You could have a strong idealistic association where you serve by bringing out your distinctly different skill sets. Virgo can learn a lot from you.

Aquarius + Libra

You are both governed by the air element and have similar attitudes to life. You are both progressive about love and romance, and Libra is probably just as committed to being non-committed as you are, Aquarius. You have a wonderful blend of energies and can learn a lot from each other.

Aquarius + Scorpio

Scorpio is all about feelings and can provide you with some of the emotional nourishment that's necessary for you. You are sensitive, but only on your own terms.

Scorpio can offer you inner satisfaction of the heart. Don't let your obstinate attitudes stand in the way of love.

Aquarius + Sagittarius

You both live your lives at breakneck speed and are concerned with fitting as much as possible into your day. If these two star signs link up, life will never be dull. You'll entertain each other, and this will become the basis for a long-term relationship.

Aquarius + Capricorn

You are opposites in nature and in almost every aspect of your lives. Capricorn needs a bit of a push to move them out of their comfort zone, whereas Aquarius could use the steady hand of Capricorn to keep them anchored in the here-and-now. Your approach to lovemaking may be a little way-out for Capricorn, so take it slowly.

Aquarius + Aquarius

You both crave excitement, change and the unusual, even the bizarre. You'll have a dramatic relationship, but you mustn't let yourselves become too self-centred. Ensure that you make time for each other while still tending to the needs of the world at large. This will be a unique experience for both of you.

Aquarius + Pisces

Pisces might have difficulty trusting you due to your aloof manner. There could also be financial issues. Hopefully, this won't be a result of taking advantage of the generous, compassionate Pisces. When it comes to money, even if you are in a long-term relationship, it might be best if you both have separate bank accounts.

PLATONIC RELATIONSHIPS: BEST AND WORST

BEST PAIRING: AQUARIUS AND GEMINI

You are off to a good start as friends because of your elementally compatible air signs. You are both extremely talented when it comes to communication and this will enable you to share your ideas as well as your feelings as friends.

To make a match work, you need compatibility. As friends, the element of air is your connectivity and allows you to relate to each other with great communication. There's no point trying to have a friendship with someone who is not on the same page, is there?

The triangular position of your star signs, according to astrology, is an excellent prophecy, not only for great friendship, but also positive future karma. You have a soul connection with Gemini and this enables you to go well beyond the intellectual aspects of communication. You can reach each other on a more intuitive level of understanding and sometimes think the same thoughts at the same time. But being almost like twins doesn't mean that you are.

You are both a bit erratic and some would even say scattered in the way you think and do things. With your mutual love of adventure, your discussions and general conversation will no doubt be about excitement and exploration. However, there may come a time, further along in your friendship, when you look back over the years and wonder what you have achieved. But does it really matter? Probably not. Aquarius and Gemini are two star signs who tend to live in the moment without laboriously planning for the future.

Having fun is high on your mutual agenda, and with a supportive and fun-loving relationship, no harm is done. You both enjoy the journey more than the destination.

It is unlikely that you will ever run out of things to talk about as your interests are varied. You are involved in so many different activities and connected on so many levels that you will enjoy each other's company before seeking out someone else to share in your discussions.

As caring and sharing individuals, you never tire of being in each other's company. What you talk about is secondary to just being together and enjoying your time with each other. That is not to say that you won't have opinions that clash, but problems in this relationship should be few and far between.

WORST PAIRING: AQUARIUS AND CANCER

Aquarians have a more intellectual attitude to life than Cancerians, who are more concerned with emotions and intuitive responses to life. This is a difference that will make this air and water sign combination difficult. You are likely to find yourselves working hard to make this pairing work, but you will keep getting dragged down because of elemental differences. You will find it almost impossible to understand why Cancer is so emotional and sensitive about everything that you say. Tiptoeing around their sensitivity is going to drive you absolutely crazy in the long run.

To keep this friendship afloat, Aquarius, you will need to be extremely adaptable to deal with their constant mood swings. Cancer is ruled by the Moon and it is one of the most emotional star signs. If you can't get into the swing of their cycles and mood changes, the relationship is doomed.

In this friendship, Cancer can be insensitive, detached and lacking in compassion. You will find that they are quite happy to blame you for everything that goes wrong and put it down to 'you just don't understand where I am coming from'. This is not true at all; you are an intellectual sign and have a whole different way of seeing things. If you are in a friendship with a Cancerian, you may need to look at how you express your emotions to improve the connection with them. Is it worth a try? That is up to you, Aquarius.

SEXUAL RELATIONSHIPS: BEST AND WORST

BEST PAIRING: AQUARIUS AND LIBRA

If you are in a relationship with a Libran, then you can count yourself very lucky indeed, Aquarius. There is a wonderful connection between these two star signs, and it is probably the best combination you will find. That is not to say that there won't be challenges along the way, but because of your wonderful ability to communicate your ideas and feelings, problems will be solved in the nicest way possible.

You are a fixed air sign, Aquarius, and this makes you a little inflexible in your thinking. Librans have the ability to be adaptable and adjust themselves to your ideas and philosophies. They also have the ability to calm your rather highly strung nature and fit in perfectly with your lifestyle. The question is, however, how will you fit in with theirs?

Librans tend to be the social butterflies of the zodiac. Their social calendar is always full and they love nothing better than to party, mix with lots of different people and flirt, which is as natural to them as breathing. You may want them to be exclusively yours, but you must be prepared for the eventuality that this may not happen.

As the ruler of the New Age, you are a progressive sign, Aquarius, and you are likely to be okay with sexual and romantic freedom—to some extent. If you are able to allow Libra the same freedom you want for yourself, then your relationship will be wonderful for you both.

A GREAT SEXUAL MATCH

From a sexual point of view, there is a lot going for this relationship. Your Libran partner is caring, affectionate and happy to explore the sexual possibilities you desire. You are able to meet each other's sexual and physical needs on many levels, which is something that will last the length of the relationship.

Mercury rules romance for Aquarius and Uranus governs Libra's romance. This planetary combination gives the relationship a youthfulness that is experimental and full of energy. The practicalities of life may intrude occasionally, and as the relationship progresses beyond pure sexual enjoyment, you will both have to adjust.

You can have great success, both individually and as a couple, as there is strong creative flair in both of you. Apart from your sexual compatibility, you are capable of stimulating great ideas in each other. Boredom is not on your sexual agenda, and this is a key ingredient in preserving the longevity of your relationship. Aquarius and Libra can have a long-lasting relationship with all the elements of a loving, playful exploration of each other's sexuality. You are two very lucky people!

WORST PAIRING: AQUARIUS AND VIRGO

It is not always a major difference that brings a relationship undone. In your case, it can be derailed before it even gets going. Virgo's precise and intellectual demands can take their toll on a relationship with Aquarius.

You are unable to relate to Virgo on an intellectual level, and their fussy hygienic ways and fastidious nature put the brakes on the free-flowing and progressive way in which you relate to someone sexually.

Although Virgo falls in the sexual zone of Aquarius, you may find that there is something about their manner that really turns you off. This will probably happen even before you get to the bedroom, and as sexuality is a deeply intimate issue, the physical act depends on the harmony of many factors for it to be fulfilling.

TOO METICULOUS

Virgo will make you feel that you just don't make the grade. Not only are they incredibly tidy and meticulous in their own environment, but they are also meticulous in the private areas of their sexual activities, which could make you wonder what on earth motivates them.

You love freedom and breaking rules, and their composed, almost cold behaviour just does not fit in with what you want from a partnership. Virgo can learn a lot from you about sex and intimacy, if they can get over their initial shock. You could help them release their tension and relax their uptight ways, but it is not something you want to do for the rest of your life, is it?

Putting so much energy into a relationship may work for a while, but you need to get something out of it as well. All this extra effort may fail to turn on your Virgo partner, and they will remain just as they are. There is certainly no problem with Virgo's cleanliness or tidiness, but sometimes these traits can be obsessive, and you could become concerned about their psychological wellbeing.

You are not ashamed of spontaneously sharing your innermost feelings with someone, but the preparation that goes into Virgo's bedtime ritual will probably drive you crazy. They want everything to be just right before they can even get around to the subject of intimacy. Unfortunately, you may have gone off the boil by the time they are clean enough and ready for intimacy.

At this stage you will wonder what attracted you to your Virgo partner in the first place. They are shy, service-orientated and usually happy to stay in the background. You may decide that there is no way you can change them—and you would be quite right. This is the reason why Aquarius and Virgo are at the bottom of the astrological compatibility list.

QUIZ: HAVE YOU FOUND YOUR PERFECT MATCH?

Are you game enough to take the following quick quiz to see how good a lover you are? The truth sometimes hurts, but it is the only way to develop your relationship skills.

It is no surprise to anyone that we are all searching for our soul mate, the modern version of the knight on a white horse or maiden in distress. In the hurly burly of life, we might bypass that special one all because we are not looking hard enough.

You may be in a relationship that started off with fireworks but that is now burnt out. When will you know if that happens and what will you do about it?

If you are in currently in a relationship, are you truly happy or just marking time until someone else comes along who suits you better? Are you content with just one partner, or would you rather play the field?

When you are without a partner, are you happy on your own or do you feel as though half of you is missing and just waiting to be joined up with someone new?

Are you in a situation where you just don't seem able to find anyone, let alone the perfect partner? Are you looking in the right places?

Aquarius, you love to serve others and give them joy. This is in keeping with your humane and charitable nature. You are also inclined to search for harmony in your friendships and love life. This isn't always an easy task for you as you fear commitment. In fact, it can take quite a long time for you to trust someone enough to fall in love with them.

So here's a checklist for you, Aquarius, to see if he or she is the right one for you.

Scoring System:

Yes = 1 point

No = 0 points

- Does your partner allow you to have your own sense of individuality?
- Do they give you a sense of freedom?
- Were you friends before you started the relationship?
- Are you good friends as well as lovers?
- Do you feel that you are 'magnetically attracted' to your partner, but can't explain why?
- Your partner doesn't dictate or assume what you are thinking, right?
- Are they smart enough to go with the flow of your wild and funny conversations?
- Do they support you and encourage you in life?
- Do they stimulate every part of your being?
- Does your partner fully trust you?
- Do they challenge you in positive ways?

- Does your partner fall under the sign of Aries, Gemini, Libra or Sagittarius?
- Do they understand and tolerate your whims and unusual ideas?
- Do they show compassion towards others?
- Are you interested in your partner's viewpoints?
- Do they share the same life ideals?

Have you been honest with your answers? Really? There is absolutely nothing to be gained here by tweaking the answers to suit the outcome. If you are aware that you are turning a blind eye to some things that are irritating or fall short of your expectations, then you will not get a real representation of your relationship.

Here are the possible points that you can score:

8 to 16 points

A good match. This shows you have obviously done something right. You have a partner who understands you, your life and your needs. But this doesn't mean you can just sit back and relax. There is always room to improve and make this excellent relationship even better.

5 to 7 points

Half-hearted prospect. You are going to need to work hard at this relationship. It may require some good honest dialogue between the two of you, and honesty is the keyword here. Go through the questions with each other and see what it is that's not allowing a better relationship to shine through. Is one of you too lazy or too domineering? After some time, do the quiz again and see if you rate your romance better. If not, it might be time to call it quits.

0 to 4 points

Washed up. There is insufficient mutual respect and understanding on this score. It's likely that neither of you is happy and that you have become too comfortable, like a worn out pair of slippers. Is that what you want to be?

2013
YEARLY OVERVIEW

LIFE'S TRAGEDY IS THAT WE GET OLD
TOO SOON AND WISE TOO LATE.

Benjamin Franklin

KEY EXPERIENCES

Due to the difficult relationship between Mars and Saturn, your frustrations in life can reach fever pitch during the first part of 2013. Although you have high expectations, others may thwart your efforts at success.

Notwithstanding these temporary hurdles, the placement of Jupiter in your lucky zone of creativity and romance should more than offset the downside of some of these planetary positions.

Your sense of responsibility is strong this year, which is reflected by Saturn's slow but testing movement in your career and self-development. You may achieve a good position, but it will come with a sacrifice. You will need to balance your personal and professional affairs in a shrewd manner.

With Uranus creating a storm in your zone of communications, you must work hard at using your creative energy in a positive and beneficial way for all. It will be too easy for you to take out your frustrations on others.

With the slow but steady movement of Jupiter in its protective mode this year, and notwithstanding some of the challenges from other planets, 2013 should bring you some positive karma and deep self-satisfaction.

ROMANCE AND FRIENDSHIP

As the year commences, you are lucky to have Venus in your zone of friendship. This indicates an active time with existing friends, but also a strong desire to extend your social network to new and exciting avenues. This is also supported by Uranus in your zone of communications, which shows that you could forge new pathways with the friends you meet—and they'll be very different from your usual style or choice.

As mentioned earlier, Jupiter has a wonderful influence on you this year, and for the first time in many years, it provides you with ample opportunities to experience positive and uplifting friendships and love affairs.

THE INFLUENCE OF MARS

The planet to be mindful of this year is Mars, whose influence directly impacts upon your marriage and most intimate relationships. You need to exercise a greater amount of self-control, even if you think you are right. Mars produces an agitated state of mind, which may cause you not to see clearly.

Furthermore, with the placement of Venus and Jupiter indicating a push for new friends and overinflated expectations, you may be too impulsive for your own good. You may choose people who are not going to necessarily bring you satisfaction in the long run. Be prudent in your choice of friends.

Due to the dominion of Venus and Jupiter over your social and romantic affairs, it is quite likely that a long-term friend may end up becoming more than that. You will need to carefully assess the consequences of taking a friendship to the next level.

Relationships on the Rise

There are key dates when your romantic affairs are likely to prosper, so it is important to understand when and how to make the most of these planetary opportunities for your star sign.

You are off to a great start in your social affairs, particularly after the 2nd of January. Venus prompts you to seek out social opportunities through workplace relationships. This will continue strongly up until the 9th when you are likely to want more one-on-one contact with others, rather than group scenarios.

Excitement is in the air after the 2nd of February when Venus enters your Sun sign. Be careful not to burn yourself out, as this is likely when Venus approaches the Sun. Yes, you will be very popular until the 26th, but don't sacrifice your health and wellbeing for the sake of a good time.

You become idealistic in March, and when Venus and Neptune make contact with each other, you are likely to make errors of judgment in your choice of partners. Around the 5th you will be wasteful with your resources and possibly try too hard to win the affection or approval of others. You don't need to try that hard to make friends.

One of the most favourable aspects for your relationships occurs on the 1st of April, when Venus and Jupiter produce loving and lucky vibrations for you. Around the 7th, Venus and Mars punctuate these energies by adding a dash of sex and sizzle to the planetary equation. This may run unabated until the 15th, when your energies will be redirected to family matters.

The 10th and 31st of May and the 2nd of June are all powerful dates that will produce excellent results for your love life. On or around the 8th of June, you will be more serious about love when Saturn tempers your passions and you are able to get down to the serious business of identifying what you and your partner want in your relationships.

Things may run fairly smoothly for you until the 2th of July, when a rather cool and difficult cycle commences in your relationships. As usual, communication is the best solution to get things back on track.

Venus produces lucky romantic results around the 17th of August, and then again on the 3rd and 14th of September. These energies gently nudge you into bigger and better professional opportunities after the 19th, which could result in some extraordinary opportunity around the 8th of October, when your deepest heartfelt desires may finally be realised.

Towards the end of the year, after the 16th of November, try to relax a little in your relationships and don't become too demanding of your partner. This could undo all the good that you have done throughout the earlier part of the year.

WORK AND MONEY

Harness Your Moneymaking Powers

Making money can be summed up in an equation:

$$m\ (\$\ \text{money}) = e\ (\text{energy}) \times t\ (\text{time}) \times l\ (\text{love})$$

If one of the elements above is not functioning properly in your life, making money may become all the more difficult. With the way the world economy is going, you need to do everything you can to improve your chances of being financially independent and secure.

It's always necessary to gain an understanding of all the universal laws of abundance and success when dealing with money. When fully present and creative, you inject the spirit of enthusiasm and love in what you do, be it work or play, and your aura or electromagnetic appeal becomes so much stronger. It is a force that attracts people, opportunities and, of course, more money. Your destiny and karma can be significantly influenced by the way you think and the attitude you foster. This will in turn impact upon your moneymaking powers.

Aquarius, I am not going to pretend that this year is going to be a bed of roses—far from that. Saturn indicates that the forecast is for intensely hard work. Yes, it will pay off in the end, but while you are plugging away at it, you could feel as if you are treading water and simply wasting your time. But you must be patient throughout 2013 for the good effects of your karma to ripen. Don't lose heart, even though excessive work may be piled on you and the sense of responsibility will weigh heavily upon your shoulders. By remaining true to your principles and the object of your desires, you will come out on top.

This year, the secret to making more money and impressing others with your abilities is 'patience'. You will have ample opportunity to show others what you can do due to the favourable position of Venus, but Mars is somewhat adverse, and even though you are hungry for recognition and success, this planet may make you a little overbearing and demanding of others, which could set you back. Gently pursue your goals and let quiet assertiveness be the energy that attracts customers, goodwill and extra money for your employer.

A CONSERVATIVE APPROACH

This year, one of the secrets of moneymaking success is being a little more conservative. This doesn't mean ditching your progressive ideas for something that is boring. Saturn tells us that a more conservative and conventional way of approaching work or presenting your ideas will reel in the success you are looking for.

After July, there are indicators that you will be working overtime. As I say to many of my clients, 'Work hard, but don't forget to work smart'. Get adequate rest, keep a clear mind and don't waste your energies on activities and projects that don't have a practical and conservative anchor attached to them.

By November, when the Sun reaches the pinnacle of your horoscope and Venus is in your profit zone, I can assure you that much of your hard work will start to pay dividends. Yes, it may seem like it is a little late in the year, but all good things come to those who wait.

Tips for Financial Success

The positioning of Mars in your finance zone after the 2nd of February can cut both ways. You have a dynamic level of energy and an appetite to earn money, but you may also spend it just as quickly. The tip here is that it isn't what you earn but what you save that amounts to future good fortune. The 10th of February is particularly important for heeding this advice as you may have a tendency to spend impulsively around this date.

Speculations are excellent after the 10th of May and up until the 14th, but this window of opportunity should be heeded with caution. By all means follow your dreams and investigate what is on offer, but don't, under any circumstances, give away money to those who haven't got proof in hand.

You are lucky in cutting a deal after the 28th of June when Venus enters your zone of partnerships and business protocols. Around the 13th of July, Mars and the Sun will overwork you. Trust this process as it will help close the deal. A very lucky time occurs after the 11th of September when Venus enters your zone of careers. Throughout this month and into October, especially after the 8th, you should start to see a nice flow of income as a result of your excellent efforts and charming ways.

Career Moves and Promotions

You have to be clever in the way that you manoeuvre yourself this year as Saturn will stand firm in your career zone, placing tests and hurdles in your way. This may seem like a negative forecast, but let me assure you that if you can overcome the destructive nature of this planet, the rewards will be greater than you could possibly imagine. Indeed, you will be tested a lot harder, placed under the microscope and given a lot more responsibility to see whether or not you can handle bigger and better jobs that are on offer.

The Sun and Saturn have an excellent relationship in the first week of March, and it is at this time that you can cautiously throw your hat in the ring for a job. You may be lucky at this time, even if you feel as though you haven't made the impression you would have liked. Remain positive under all circumstances. You will probably find good news relating to a job interview arriving after the 7th of March.

March is an important month because Mars enters the zone of contract, making this an important time for you to request changes in your current work status or to sign a new workplace agreement. This will take place after the 12th.

The eclipse on the 26th of April reveals much about your work, but more about your desire to achieve something meaningful in the world. Investigate your true motivation for work, and if you are not doing something that fulfils you, it could be time to make a major change. On the 10th of May, another eclipse in your zone of family and home life could indicate a need to balance these two parts of your life more carefully so you find peace and satisfaction in work and family life as well.

Some of your deepest professional dreams may be achieved after the 19th of July when Saturn and Neptune enter into a very favourable aspect. Remember, you must keep some of your dreams practical. Asking for a new job or going for an interview becomes easier after the 11th of September when Venus enters the tenth house. Fulfilment can be expected around the 8th of October.

The rest of the year should be a little smoother, or at least easier to handle, when this planet brings with it a sense of ease and self-confidence.

When to Avoid Office Politics

You must be careful this year because your enemies may actually befriend you. You may not be aware that this is happening, and you could mistake adversaries for those who wish to do you good. This is a terrible thing to be told because it makes it hard for you to trust anyone. I am not advising you to distrust people, but calculated investigation, straight-to-the-point questioning and a not-too-gullible attitude will spare you much heartache when it comes to people undermining you and competitively trying to get you out of the picture.

Because Saturn is considered your secret enemy as well as your ruling planet, it is important to point out that some office politics you wish to avoid may actually be instigated by your subconscious. In other words, you could be your own worst enemy this year.

Some of the dates when you should be more aware of your behaviour, attitude and the words that you use in your office or workplace are the 8th of March, the 22nd of April, the 6th of May and the 21st of June. It is best to say less rather than diving into quicksand. Once a word has left your lips, it is almost impossible to take it back.

You may need to deal with some open enmity between the 13th and the 19th of October. I mentioned earlier that some of your enemies may be hidden, but during this cycle and towards the end of the year, the identity of those who wish to do you ill may be clearly known.

HEALTH, BEAUTY AND LIFESTYLE

Venus Calendar for Beauty

This year, Venus blesses you with exciting social opportunities, but doesn't it make sense to look and feel your best to make the most of the opportunities that are presented to you?

After the 7th of February, take some extra time to study the colour, harmony and symmetry of your face, as well as the way you use makeup. During this phase, when Venus is in your Sun sign, you can make a wonderful impression on others, even though Mars may cause you to overdo things.

SUBTLE BEAUTY

Don't exaggerate your features. It's better to enhance them in a delicate but personal way when trying to share your beauty with others. Downplaying your beauty will bring you wonderful success.

You must hydrate your skin this year. With Mars having an important say in your physical vitality at the start of the year, you may find your skin lacking in moisture. Mars is a hot and dry planet, and moving through your Sun sign, in conjunction with the Sun, can actually dehydrate you more than you think. Drink lots of water and keep your skin and pores open. This allows a better aeration and free flow of energy through your skin. This method will enable you to glow and further impress others with your beautiful aura.

The triangular and angular positions of Venus highlight the power to do good in your life, and on the 10th of May the 28th of June, the 17th of August and, very importantly, the 11th of September, you must utilise the energies of this friendly planet to showcase your good looks, graceful attitude and intelligence. Yes, intelligence is an inner form of beauty and it is essential to win over the hearts of others.

Venus takes you to great heights after the 27th of October when it enters the zone of friendship, bringing with it all sorts of positive karmic returns. Your beauty will be well noted at this time as well.

Showing off Your Aquarian Traits

Each Zodiac sign has its own unique power based upon the elements and planets that rule it. Unfortunately, most people don't know how to tap into this power to bring out their greatest potential to achieve success in life.

Previously, Saturn was your ruler, but the modern ruler of your star sign is Uranus. In 2013, both these planets occupy the star sign of Aries.

There is an exchange between Mars and Uranus, your ruler, which indicates that you have the opportunity to strongly showcase your drive, ambition and intellect. You can do this throughout January and February, when you will be able to articulate your feelings and viewpoints much more strongly.

Because your older ruler, Saturn, is in Scorpio, this brings with it a sensual and even sexual flavour to your personality, which people may not often identify with Aquarius. You can definitely dig deep into that arsenal of sensual and magnetic energies and use it to good advantage in 2013, especially in your workplace, where icy Saturn stands firm throughout the next year or so. Putting on the charm will counteract these Saturnine influences.

Passion is very different to aggression, and you must allow others to see the passion, warmth and sexual energy that are possible for those born under the sign of Aquarius. Approaching life this way will bring added and unexpected benefits.

Best Ways to Celebrate

There is no doubt that you will want to celebrate and share your joys and special events with others in the early part of the year. However, this will change by around the end of April or May, when Venus, the planet of love and socialising, moves through your zone of family. At this time, it is best to consider celebrations in a more cloistered environment with people you love and trust. This is definitely a more intimate period, but by no means less passionate.

In May and June, your celebrations will involve one-on-one candlelit dinners that highlight true love. During this period of the year, when Mars, the Sun, Jupiter, Venus and Mercury congregate in such an important part of your horoscope, you will want to celebrate the joy of life, and, if you are in love, the bliss of being with a soul mate. This should be an extraordinarily happy period for you.

Aquarius Loves to Party

If you celebrate your birthday, anniversary or any other important event, it's important for friends and loved ones to understand that the Aquarian temperament is partial to big and fun-filled events where they can share their excitement and love. Generally, Aquarians love to party hard, laugh heartily and go to extremes.

Celebrations take an interesting turn after August and through September when Venus works its magic in your zone of long-distance journeys, education and spiritual pursuits. As strange as it seems, these could be areas that bring you great joy, and in the company of others with similar views or intentions, it can be a time when your joy is shared in a group situation that has intellectual and cultural benefits for you.

KARMA, SPIRITUALITY AND EMOTIONAL BALANCE

Mercury and Venus are important for Aquarians as they represent the past and the future. Your good, bad or indifferent karma will come to fruition when these planets make important connections in your horoscope. This year, you are lucky socially and financially due to the placement of Venus, your past karmic influence, in your zone of fulfilment. But the most important connections between these two planets occur throughout the middle of May and June, and it is at this time that your positive karma will come to light.

This is not only an important karmic period for 'receiving things or people', but a time when you can see clearly within you. It is hard to explain exactly how this may manifest, but it is akin to understanding one's life purpose—one of the most difficult things for any of us to discover. You will be blessed with a clear picture of who you are, what you wish to be and how you can make your mark in this world.

Venus enters your zone of future karma on the 10th of May, so this is a good time to unfurl your sails and allow the winds of destiny to carry you forward creatively and romantically. Conversely, when Venus enters your ninth zone of past karma on the 17th of August, you will be looking back and trying to clarify what you have done and how it has led you here. All of these things are perfect in the scheme of improving your life, finding your spiritual destiny and becoming a fully integrated human being.

2013
MONTHLY & DAILY PREDICTIONS

A YEAR FROM NOW YOU WILL WISH
YOU HAD STARTED TODAY.

Karen Lamb

JANUARY

Monthly Highlight

You are likely to be reactive due to the strong presence of Mars in your rising sign. You are emotional about relationships and have a strong sense that you should be experiencing more from your partner. Be careful not to be too demanding, or your requests could backfire. Troublesome times in relationships can be pinpointed on the 8th, the 13th and the 26th of January. At these times, try to be more receptive to the needs of your partner rather than superimposing your own fears and expectations on them.

1 Get to the point rather than expecting people to understand you. You may be scared of not being accepted for your ideas. Bravery is your keyword today.

2 Initiate a new hobby or take up some study with a view to learning something new. A talk could be inspiring.

3 You mustn't feel defeated if you're losing ground financially. These are the ups and downs of life and there will be an improvement shortly.

4 You'll be enchanted at a get-together with old friends or travellers. You could feel somewhat excitable due to Mercury and Uranus.

5 You have some great concepts and energy right now, but you need to make them practical and apply them to your everyday experiences.

6 Use your creative abilities to improve your surroundings. Be forward-thinking in the way you recreate your living space to produce more harmony in your life.

7 You need to give some time to yourself and pat yourself on the back for a job well done. Today you should acknowledge yourself rather than beat yourself up.

8 You will get the recognition you deserve for the efforts you've put into your friendships. Receiving credit is important.

9 Too many people may make you feel uncomfortable today. Don't just grin and bear it. Get away from everyone if that's what you want.

10 Today you may be given advice by well-meaning friends and relatives, but in the end your own instincts will prevail.

11 Create your own timetable and enjoy your day. The kitchen, garden and other home hobbies can be just as satisfying as expensive pastimes.

12 This is a time when your physical vitality may not be very high, so take a moderate approach to work and exercise.

13 You are more emotionally expressive than usual, but you need to control your feelings, otherwise you will be overwhelmed.

14 You have a strange sense that something is missing, concealed or removed from your immediate environment. Detective-like work is necessary for you to get to the bottom of things.

15 If you're confused about your finances at the moment, you need to go back over the original receipts and check for errors.

16 Travelling and moving about will bring you happiness today. Resolving problems should be on your agenda now, but a journey may be involved.

17 You may have to come down on someone if they breach the rules of etiquette. But don't let that awkward moment ruin an event.

18 Your positive state of mind can have a beneficial effect on friends and family members right now. It may seem easier than usual to be nice today.

19 Some younger people may have the answers you've been seeking about a certain situation. Listen and take their opinions on board.

20 You could be presented with an opportunity that seems too good to be true. This may be the case, but it is still worthwhile investigating.

21 You can now understand where things are not quite right and may even uncover some dishonesty around you. Be careful how you approach the subject.

22 Discipline is needed if you want to maintain relationships. Get involved in your partner's life.

23 You may have a preview of what's to come in your life because you are more intuitive right now. Fortunately, you can correct your actions if you see something negative.

24 Romance is indispensable to a good relationship. You need to actively seek it rather than complain about not having it.

25 You could be the recipient of good news today, but you may not be able to act upon it as quickly as you'd like. Patience is your keyword just now.

26 You could feel larger than life right now. Be careful not to extend your generosity without discrimination; you may overlook characters on the take.

27 The day could be emotionally gruelling. You mustn't allow others to press your buttons.

28 You may have to offer an apology for the sake of harmony. The only thing getting in the way is your ego.

29 You need to play the role of seductress if someone questions your abilities in the bedroom. This could be fun.

30 You'll need to deal with family issues right now. The manner in which you handle this, especially if it is impartial, will be appreciated.

31 A friend's legal issues could weigh down your friendship. It is best to not get too involved in other people's personal problems.

FEBRUARY

Monthly Highlight

With the Sun in your sign, you can feel energised and physically motivated, and when Venus enters your sign on the 2nd, your social instincts will be at their peak.

Be mindful of financial problems after the 5th, when Mars and Neptune create some confusion in this area of your life. The position of Saturn in your career zone indicates some rather intense responsibilities that you may need to work through.

1 It would be useful to start showing off your talents right now. Don't let it go to your head if people start complimenting you on your abilities.

2 Don't be afraid to ask for help. Friends will be helpful, even if you feel reluctant to ask them.

3 You should keep abreast of new people in your workplace or social circle. They may not be what they seem, so study them carefully beforehand.

4 You can share concepts, put forward bold new plans and get the support you need from others. Execute your ideas today.

5 You may be intolerant of certain foods and medications today. Be careful what you ingest.

6 You have a strong connection with your relatives and friends today and want to show your affection more strongly. Don't overdo it.

7 If you've been working hard on a project that has been tedious, you can expect the going to get easier today.

8 You could feel bighearted and will devote some time looking for a gift for someone special. Remember, the gift doesn't have to be expensive; it's the thought that counts.

9 Let go of the past if it's still affecting you. Don't let it ruin your peace of mind.

10 You could be wasteful with your spending today as Mars and Jupiter indicate the likelihood of little or no impulse control. Be mindful of costs.

11 You mustn't be duped by clever words. This is a sly ploy to reel you in, so be cautious when dealing with others.

12 If you've forgotten a close friend lately due to work commitments, get out that address book and start phoning or emailing.

13 You could be feeling negative because of what you haven't achieved rather than looking at the positive outcome.

14 Don't lose control of your emotions when negotiating with your boss. Understanding and communication will conquer all. You just need to look a bit deeper for answers.

15 If you're home- or job-hunting, you could find success in the form of an offer or referral. Settle for no less than what you believe is fair! Do research online.

16 You have a great deal of imagination just now and someone may be envious of this. But remember, you don't need to justify your creativity.

17 A constructive attitude will help you achieve a great deal today. Don't be distracted by people who are flippant and less focused.

18 Enjoy something a little different today, even if you risk ridicule. You'll enjoy yourself and also provide enjoyment to someone else.

19 Friends may turn into enemies and vice versa today. This could confuse you. Go back and redefine what you mean by friendship.

20 You need to look carefully at your health and see whether you have been helping your body achieve optimal wellbeing. Investigate.

21 Have no fear in taking on a new project, even if you feel it's out of your depth. Your confidence should be strong just now.

22 You may not be open in your dealings with others, mainly due to self-preservation. Others may try to use you or your ideas.

23 Stop relying on others for your success in life. Become more independent and develop self-confidence in your abilities.

24 Your craving for love is so strong that you could be making wrong choices. Your moods may also be subject to hormonal fluctuations.

25 You want to gain someone's attention right now. Once they know you're around, you can take the friendship to the next level.

26 You can support your capacity to earn with your knowledge of finance. You may also need to act as a teacher to others who aren't as knowledgeable, but you can learn from them as well.

27 More assertive communication is needed right now. Practice makes perfect.

28 Don't share your philosophical or political opinions unless asked. This could create antagonism among your circle of friends.

MARCH

Monthly Highlight

You are idealistic this month as Venus and Neptune combine in transit. This will not only affect your romantic affairs, but also your finances and family relationships. You will need to see things as they are, rather than as you imagine them.

Some travel is indicated after the 20th, when the Sun moves through your zone of short journeys. Venus also activates this area of your horoscope after the 22nd. Be careful to plan well ahead of time. Mars and Uranus could create some sudden obstructions or mishaps around the 23rd.

1 Additional expenses influence your capacity to enjoy the moment. You need to take into consideration other expenses that haven't yet arrived.

2 Even if your clothes are outdated, you can still be attractive. The biggest part of attractiveness is personality.

3 You needn't put up with the demands of people who give little in return. Don't be afraid to ask for mutual exchange.

4 Friends could be sending mixed messages today. You'll need to get clarification on what they mean.

5 You may initiate a new friendship, but you shouldn't do this out of pity because the person is having a hard time.

6 If you continually agree with everyone to make them happy, you will be hiding your true self. Be brutally honest, even at the expense of losing a friend.

7 An unexpected call could bring positive benefits. It could be an old friend or someone you haven't seen for a while.

8 Step outside your tightly knit circle of friends and relatives and meet someone new. This is a good time to be daring and curious.

9 You may find that things at home are not quite to your liking. Stay calm and ask others to pitch in and help.

10 A planned vacation or day out with a friend may have to be changed or postponed. Have an alternative plan in the wings.

11 Don't let someone ruffle your feathers today if the conversation gets out of hand. Maintain your composure.

12 You could be chained to a situation and need to break free. It may have something to do with an illicit or dead love affair.

13 You may have great financial obligations right now, but if you attack them with a positive, can-do attitude, you will come out a winner.

14 You could get sucked into an emotional storm if you're not careful. If others choose to quarrel, give them space and don't interfere.

15 Expect an intense telephone call that may leave you drained. Cut the call short if necessary.

16 The tried and tested is your security blanket today, but you need to move beyond that. Look further afield to develop yourself.

17 Your home life could be a little frustrating right now. You need to explore ways in which you can improve the situation.

18 You need to postpone or change your plans for a vacation or holiday. Have a plan B ready.

19 Meetings today could be somewhat tedious, so it's up to you to inject a bit of lightheartedness into the situation.

20 Looking for a new house? You need to explore alternative ways of finding the best deal in the marketplace.

21 Because you are distracted, you may find that there is something amiss in your finances. The secret is to keep your mind focused today.

22 You may have concerns about a friend's behaviour, but how will they ever change if you don't tell them? Be brave.

23 Don't overdo your exercise regime as this can do more harm than good. Moderation is your key right now.

24 If you'd like to feel young again, you need to do things that are more youthful than what you are currently doing. It also means that you may need to hang out with younger people.

25 If you don't feel as if you have an adequate body, why complain? How you look and feel is your responsibility.

26 Saving money is one thing, but if what you buy falls apart too quickly, what's the point?

27 You could be shocked at the exploding cost of some items right now! Either cut back on these expenses or find a way of earning more money.

28 You need to activate a friendship by making a call. If you're waiting for them, you could be waiting a long time.

29 If a reason needs to be given to someone, make it short and sweet. If you elaborate, you could be there for a long time.

30 You need to get off the beaten track today and find some quiet time in nature. This is the only way you'll get some sanity.

31 If you're asking someone to diagnose or fix something, make sure they're qualified to do so.

APRIL

Monthly Highlight

You need to escape right now and could feel frustrated by the demands of your employer or workplace. Uranus, the Sun, Venus and Mars challenge your sense of commitment. Balancing work and pleasure will be your challenge this month. Excellent opportunities to resolve some of your problems occur after the 25th, but the time leading up to this may be less than satisfactory for you.

1 Today is a day when work projects will occupy your mind. You will have little time to do anything else. Try to find a balance between work and play.

2 Sometimes, being alone is the only way you can get a solution. Don't rely on others to show you the way; look within yourself.

3 The decisions you make during this time may have important relevance to the future outcome of your work. This indicates a happy and prosperous cycle.

4 You may receive settlement on some sort of payment or debt. Profit shares and the stock market will also be beneficial to you during this period.

5 You may call someone out for being unethical. Others may judge you harshly, but you have your own reasons for acting this way.

6 You wish to raise your consciousness and seek out spiritual activities and mentors. This is an important phase in your development.

7 You could be completely burned-out from work, which means you need to ask yourself whether or not you are happy with what you are doing.

8 You will be tested and find yourself under a lot of pressure. The trick is to relax and not react too strongly to what is being thrown at you.

9 Don't be a sucker to those who want to use you financially. You could experience some sort of loss if you are not diligent.

10 Your partner may not be doing their bit to support you. You feel as if you are carrying the weight of everyone else on your shoulders. Only you can change this.

11 You are in a state of suspension because you don't know what is happening. You need to be patient. As events unfold, they will be likely to turn out in your favour.

12 Your social appetite is strong today, so you will need the company of good people who can connect with you on your level. Seek them out.

13 You can start a new project at home, which will beautify your residence and living space. This is a creative day, so make the most of it.

14 You may receive a call from a distant relative. There could also be a short trip related to this. It's a relaxing time for you.

15 You may be concerned about some physical condition, but it is likely to be in your mind. Nonetheless, have it checked it out.

16 There may be a stop/start effect on your income just now. You could be waiting on some payout, and this delay will frustrate you. You may need to make some calls.

17 If unresolved personal or business issues are weighing heavily upon you, take some action now and resolve them. Why wait?

18 If you are bored with your work right now, rest assured that this is a passing phase. A new and exciting project will shortly lift your spirits.

19 You have to perform a juggling act between your work and personal commitments. This will be hard, but you can do it.

20 You may overlook something important and kick yourself over it. You need to be more diligent with the way you manage your schedule.

21 Things may not go to plan today, but rest assured that the universe is perfect in its planning. Consider the possibilities and put a positive spin on what happens today.

22 You may feel mistreated or taken for granted in a relationship, but you've only got yourself to blame. Start changing things now.

23 You may think that a relationship has finished, but you will be surprised to see it revived. If you are feeling lonely, that will change shortly.

24 You want to be more successful now, but you need to move slowly and surely. Although things look precarious just now, you are on track.

25 To alleviate your boredom today, you may decide to go on a shopping spree. This therapy can make you feel good until you receive the next credit card bill.

26 You may start to feel as if your home is no longer appealing because it has outlived its purpose. You could be looking for somewhere new to live.

27 You could have trouble with household appliances just now, so it is best to remember that purchasing cheap items is a recipe for future problems.

28 You may change your perspective on work based on new information that is given to you. This will bring with it some hope for a better future.

29 You could feel as if you have a problem, but the issue is with someone else who is projecting it onto you. Don't become the victim in this game.

30 To free yourself from a situation, you need to be vocal and let someone know exactly how you feel. Otherwise, things will stay the same.

MAY

Monthly Highlight

With no less than five planets occupying your zone of domestic activities, home affairs top the agenda this month. There may be construction, renovation and redecoration as part of your schedule. An eclipse in this area also indicates that you may need to clear out any skeletons from the closet, especially those that relate to parents, siblings or other relatives.

1 You will see the many similarities between you and another friend—and how your lives are now diverging.

2 You want to move ahead unobstructed, but someone may be getting in the way. Don't keep it to yourself; share your grievances.

3 You may fear that you are spending less and less time with the person you love, which means you have to reappraise the relationship. Set aside some time to explain your position.

4 If you are single and have met a new potential lover, take the initiative and call them, even if you think that it may be a little embarrassing. It's time to act.

5 Your popularity may be a burden in disguise. You are working efficiently in your career, but you are now needed for other tasks. It may be time to increase your fees.

6 Someone from your past may hold the solution to a problem you are now experiencing. Don't be afraid to share your experiences with them.

7 You may not know how to act after receiving positive news at work. It can be scary, especially if it instigates change.

8 A proposed endeavour may seem exciting, but the question is, do you have time to do it?

9 Try taking your partner somewhere different. A refreshing change can revitalise your relationship and bring you joy.

10 A friend's white lie may cause you to mistrust them. It will be difficult for them to win back your favour.

11 If you are single and longing for love, you may be waiting a while longer. Consider those who don't seem absolutely perfect.

12 Because your heart is not in your work today, it is best to step aside and do something else until your enthusiasm is back on track.

13 Your family is more supportive than you think, so share your ambitions and ideas with them. You'd be surprised at just how much they will be able to help you.

14 You are overdoing certain aspects of your life, which will affect your physical wellbeing. Listen to your body's signals to regain your health.

15 You are worrying too much about money rather than trusting the universe. Focus on what you want, not on what you don't have.

16 A relationship may come to an end, but this just the beginning of things to come. When one door closes, another opens.

17 If you're not saying what you really mean, help people understand you. Be more explicit in your requests today.

18 You could feel stabbed in the back right now, and loyalty will be uppermost in your mind. You need to sift out the genuine from the fake.

19 Expect delays with government bureaucracy or other utility departments. You may have paid a bill, but you are now expected to pay it again.

20 You may be troubled by some communication breakdown that has to do with faulty communication devices. Make sure you service your equipment regularly.

21 Someone may expect a commitment from you, but this is premature. You need more time and should tell them so.

22 There will be a change in plans that a family member cannot handle alone. They may expect too much from you.

23 This is the end of negative period, and a project that has been on hold can now start again.

24 You may have said yes to too many people and will now feel the pressure of the workload you have brought upon yourself. Learn the value of the word 'no'.

25 If something seems too good to be true, it probably is. Be wary of an offer that is way too generous.

26 Your intuition is strong today, and some of your forecasts will prove to be correct. Apply this to your own life.

27 Something you are looking for may be right under your nose. Exhaust all avenues before spending money.

28 You could have an unexpected encounter with someone, but it may be short-lived. Don't place too much emphasis on new acquaintances.

29 It's time to take a break from your work, possibly in the form of long-service leave or a holiday. If you do so, make it as far away from friends and relatives as possible.

30 You may need to consult a family friend who is undergoing some personal hardship. Your compassion will assist them.

31 Dealing with uncomfortable issues requires proper timing. Today is not the day to handle problems that will drive you to distraction.

JUNE

Monthly Highlight

This is likely to be an important month for understanding deeper issues, ferreting out secrets and working on things in private. Pluto and Mercury make you investigative, detective-like, in many areas of your life.

Your zone of love affairs and creativity is also nicely activated through the presence of Mars, the Sun, Jupiter and Venus. This means that after the 6th you will be looking at meeting new people or at least taking your existing relationships to a new level.

After the 19th, you may feel somewhat disillusioned by work, but this may only be a temporary state of mind.

1 You need to sit tight and wait until a clear direction is revealed to you. What you really want will arrive.

2 You are quite restless today, so it is best to be out and about blowing off steam and getting rid of your pent-up energy. It will do you the world of good.

3 Your partner may have unforeseen problems, so most of your time will be spent serving them rather than looking after your own needs.

4 You could hear some news about someone who is not well or who needs your help in a medical way. Consolation may be the only help you can give them.

5 Someone could challenge you to step things up a notch today, but this is all good. You will embrace this new attitude as a means of furthering your success.

6 The focus today is on your career and improving the situation in your workplace. You may have some opposition to this, but you must persist.

7 Uncomfortable changes and fluctuating moods will punctuate the day. Try not to react too strongly to unrealistic demands.

8 You have to sort out some legal papers today or matters that have been swept under the rug. Don't delay things any further.

9 Don't allow emotional issues to cloud your judgment and work. You need to segregate the two.

10 Partnering is a good way to overcome excessive costs these days. Take the opportunity to share with someone else.

11 If you've been following rules and feeling upset at work, generate your own rules. You can now create new standards.

12 A temporary blockage is being caused by your resistance to change. Analyse the deeper reasons for this.

13 You may be feeling quite physical today and need an outlet in the form of sport or other competitive activities. Your creative energies are also strong.

14 You are going to find out some information that is very refreshing. This could also indicate an unanticipated social invite.

15 Big decisions require immense courage and trust in yourself. This is a new cycle of transformation, both in your personal relationships and in the way you pool your resources.

16 The way you think and act is going through a cycle of change. These are critical times and they require patience and understanding.

17 You can spend and enjoy more cash right now. Commence that new commercial plan and expect considerable wealth to flow from it.

18 If respect is what you're after, the law of the universe requires you to show it to others first. This seems like a contradiction, but it works.

19 Make adjustments to another person's viewpoint, especially if it needs to be included in the work you are doing. Don't be a spendthrift today.

20 Be ready to move quickly on a legal matter that comes to light. Dynamic discussions will motivate a legal agent or solicitor to complete your request.

21 You can't be responsible for what everyone else is doing right now, but that's exactly what is happening. You can only take responsibility for your own thoughts, words and actions.

22 An ignorant and cowardly remark from someone leaves you high and dry, but it also makes you much stronger. Use this to gain greater understanding and help others in similar situations.

23 There may be an opportunity to connect with a group of people for a reunion or family get-together.

24 Be careful of overstating your case or pushing your brilliant ideas too hard. Overselling yourself is as disadvantageous as underselling.

25 Your energy is diffused and scattered at the moment. If you have been living it up, you may be living it up too much!

26 A battle of wills may occur today, but you have more friends than you know what to do with, so this won't trouble you.

27 Continue daydreaming; it will definitely satisfy your inner desires right now. Create what you want.

28 You are deliberate and focused on some matter of communication. Be articulate in presenting your case as the outcome could mean more money for you.

29 Any self-doubts you have must be overcome if you're to move forward in your present relationship. Fears should be cast aside.

30 Visitors may annoy at a time when you need quiet time alone. Don't be afraid to say no.

JULY

Monthly Highlight

You are particularly focused on work right now and will be dreaming of bigger and better things. But first things first, Aquarius. You need to systematically work through your workload and your objectives to figure out exactly what you want. However, due to the influence of Venus and Uranus, you may be quite scattered, and focusing on these objectives won't be easy.

The period between the 18th and the 22nd is an excellent time to make good on your plans and be practical in all affairs. Financial matters, particularly those relating to savings and superannuation, need to be addressed.

---

1 Your plan to go out with someone may change and you could end up going alone. There may be some miscommunication.

---

2 A wolf in sheep's clothing may be near you. Remain alert and read between the lines when dealing with others today.

3 You can't make your mind up today because your head and your heart are not in tune. You need to create some inner harmony.

4 Improved relationships are assured right now. Sometimes, conventional circumstances and people who seem out of step with your ideas may have something valuable to offer you.

5 You have a desire to explore domestic alternatives. Look around, but don't make any rash decisions.

6 You are feeling secure in your relationships, but this is no excuse to become a couch potato. Get out and enjoy the world with your partner, if you have one.

7 There's no use crying over spilt milk, or, in your case, lost relationships. Learn from your errors. Read the character of others to learn about them.

8 Spiritual practices offer you an opportunity to recharge your worn batteries and understand why things are the way they are.

9 If you've got some concern with a friend, lover or child, these problems should be lifting very shortly.

10 You will be the victor in an argument and gain the advantage over someone. Use this as an opportunity to improve your relationship.

11 You should commence your day with meditation and exercise. This will produce a great deal of energy and help you handle your stress levels.

12 You could take control of some aspect of your work, making you more accountable in the job.

13 Domestic circumstances could spiral out of control and your emotional involvement could inflame the situation even more.

14 Don't be disheartened if you need to start something all over again. There are some lessons you need to learn through this process.

15 Never throw pearls before swine. Sharing your subtle, emotional and creative gems of wisdom with others is wasted if they are insensitive and uninterested in the more refined values of life.

16 Due to mistrust, you may shut out friends. Open the door of your heart and see who is waiting for you today.

17 Don't let your emotions dictate a course of action when it comes to employment or money. Your first reaction to news in your workplace is exaggerated. See things as they are.

18 You could be explosive today if you don't watch yourself. Events could get out of control and your reaction may be over-the-top.

19 Friendships may be in for a rocky ride because you are not in the mood to listen to a hard-luck or sob story.

20 Tensions can ease off, but not without a great deal of discipline on your part. Mercury and Uranus are the culprits today.

21 You could have a few sleepless nights worrying about something that you have no control over. At some point you will have to relinquish control.

22 An activity or business you are involved in is going nowhere. Don't stay there for the sake of it. Leave.

23 If you don't trust yourself, then your partner won't trust you either. You need to make some bold moves today to prove that you do.

24 Don't misinterpret what true power really is. Do you think that throwing your weight around and stomping on those who are in an inferior position is true strength?

25 What you imagine yourself to be is not how others see you. Your imagination is powerful now, and thinking the best of yourself is part of it.

26 You may not be your sparkling self today, but you will not want to divulge the reason. This is okay. You mustn't feel any pressure to speak about personal matters, even if someone pushes you.

27 Getting back into a hobby or pleasurable activity that you cast aside for a long while will bring you great satisfaction.

28 You might feel a little down about your romantic life today. This is because you're focusing on the negative rather than the positive.

29 Misunderstandings could be made worse if you talk in circles. Put your problems aside for a day or two until the situation settles.

30 If you are not connecting with your partner as much as you would like, a silent approach could do the trick, even though it could make you feel a little sad.

31 Share good news with your partner. They will feel included in your good fortune, which will create goodwill between you.

AUGUST

Monthly Highlight

You may have trouble remaining focused during the first week of the month as Mars and Uranus create a sudden and unexpected outburst, either from you or others. Peace can once again be had by the 17th thanks to Venus and the Sun. But by the 21st, once again, the influence of Uranus may destabilise many of your activities and, most importantly, your mind. Meditation, willpower, focus and keeping to yourself are advisable.

1 Your intellectual and verbal skills are heightened right now. Although you can make a great impression on someone at a meeting or lunch engagement, be wary if their flattery is over the top.

2 A disappointment in love doesn't mean you're out of the game permanently. This is a day to regroup and get yourself back on track.

3 It is possible that travel expenses may be covered by your place of employment or organisation. Financial aid proves beneficial.

4 You are curious about the world and want more interaction, perhaps through the internet.

5 Passive aggression will never get you anywhere. In fact, if you build up these negative emotions for too long, it will impact upon your physical health as well.

6 Create a situation in which you can get work done uninterrupted and at length. Patchy or ad-hoc work routines will undermine your efforts.

7 Don't offend anyone who is not able to keep up with your jokes. Be sensitive to the feelings of others when sharing a risqué story.

8 Someone may disappear from your life unexpectedly. Will you take this personally? It's best to be philosophical about these things.

9 An impulsive romantic escapade could turn out to be a bigger drama than you had anticipated. Check your facts and talk to friends for clarity.

10 All things connected with travel, education and legal matters are high on your agenda. Negotiate the best deal you can.

11 If there are unsettled feelings in your relationship, talk about what is on your mind. You mustn't indulge any negativity today.

12 You're feeling frustrated by someone in your professional life. If there's nothing you can do, it's best to completely forget about it.

13 People may comment that your looks or mood are different. You realise that you are going through dramatic changes.

14 Don't be afraid to ask for what you want in your workplace. If things aren't right, speak out and change may occur.

15 Your peer group at work is better informed about something than you are. Humble yourself and ask them to bring you up to speed.

16 Unwanted attention is a problem for you just now. You could feel self-conscious, perhaps about your weight or some aspect of your physical self. Rectify it.

17 You could hear rumours that are not altogether true and may feel a little rattled.

18 If you are in an educational program, you could receive some distinction in an exam.

19 You will be pleased that someone has called, but may be too busy to make the most of the event.

20 Whatever you do will be brilliant and captivate the imagination of others. This is not a time to shrink back from situations that require an authoritative hand.

21 You may take a calculated risk, which could cause financial loss. Don't overestimate your luck today.

22 Unlike yesterday, you have an opportunity to earn or win something. Be appreciative of gains, even small ones.

23 Don't go making business plans without thoroughly investigating the consequences first. Consult those nearest to you.

24 Feelings of jealousy, envy and anger might erode a good relationship. You should overcome these feelings quickly.

25 Stop burying your feelings. Although a family member may not want to hear what you have to say, it's essential for you to force the issue.

26 It's not a good idea for you to burn the candle at both ends just now. Regroup, prioritise and use your diary to manage your time, even at social get-togethers.

27 This is a day of luck for the simple reason that you are out of the limelight. Work behind the scenes.

28 You may take new risks and do things you wouldn't have attempted otherwise. Things seem to gravitate to you at the moment, which will turn out to be very beneficial.

29 You will forcibly shift yourself into a better frame of mind, which will benefit the group. You also feel a sense of inner power for doing so.

30 Temperance is your keyword today, so you will need to monitor your desire to overdo things. This extends to pleasures, such as eating and drinking.

31 It's quite likely that you can restore balance, but the first step to equilibrium is your own mental stability.

SEPTEMBER

Monthly Highlight

The New Moon is in your eighth zone of transformation, which means that it will be a transformative month. Sexual matters may be an underlying problem as evidenced by Mars transiting through your marital zone. Unless you speak about these issues, they will only snowball and get worse. The tough aspect between Mars and Saturn on the 9th will bring things to a head. You can expect some interesting times professionally as Venus adds a touch of social pleasure to your career activities.

1 A meeting with work colleagues could trigger feelings of low self-confidence and not being good enough.

2 You may connect with people you've kept at arm's length for some time. They have more in common with you than you had first thought.

3 You may be the bearer of bad news for someone. As usual, their first response is to shoot the messenger. Wear your bullet-proof vest today.

4 You might find that your employer is way too orthodox for your taste just now. You will need to drag someone into the 21st century.

5 There's nothing worse than a deaf extremist, especially when you're rationally trying to explain your side of things. You need to deal with someone like this today.

6 You may have a transient impulse today, but don't be overtaken by it. You will feel stronger by not succumbing to temptation.

7 Someone will show you care and attention, which is something you had not anticipated. A new friendship can commence.

8 You have your way of doing things, and this could be at odds with someone around you, possibly even your boss. Compromise is your keyword.

9 Home is where the heart is. You may have made a domestic change recently without thinking it through. If you've found yourself in an environment in which you feel like a fish out of water, you need to reconsider your options.

10 If you seem to be spending more time than your workmates on the same tasks, they could be working smarter. Check it out.

11 You need to quicken the pace and be more efficient in the way you conduct your work and live your life. Reappraise the way you use your diary and time.

12 You'll be feeling withdrawn today, but this gives you a chance to truly 'inhabit' your purpose and believe in it totally. Convincing others means convincing yourself first.

13 If you see that something is flawed, you may have to reverse a decision or payment. Be on guard for scam artists.

14 There may be some controversial matters you have to deal with, which could result in a conflict of interest. Try to be a step ahead of the game as the situation could take you into the unexpected.

15 You could be riding high socially, but be careful that you don't invite envy or displeasure from others. Keep a low profile.

16 Believe it or not, your anxiety could trigger a search for answers that you now need. There is a solution amongst the silly noise of the world around you.

17 You are quick to make a judgment today, but possibly too quick, and you may regret your hasty decision. Fortunately, a friend may intervene and help you see the error of your ways.

18 Don't go making business plans without thoroughly investigating the consequences first. Consult those nearest to you.

19 Making a connection with someone from your past requires some research. Your intuition tells you that you must make contact, so don't give up until the connection happens.

20 Make sure your philosophy supports your lifestyle in a practical way. Good food and exercise will also help.

21 Don't feel defeated by a lack of profit in your business or commercial ventures just now. The ups and downs of life apply to moneymaking as well.

22 Get back to basics today, even if it is more time-consuming. This will make you much more efficient in the long run.

23 It won't be easy calling on someone today because there could be some embarrassing circumstances surrounding the discussion. Be honest.

24 Things will be worse if you resume a relationship based on the thought that the person has improved. This isn't the case.

25 Sometimes you have to make unpopular decisions, but if your intentions are pure, people will ultimately understand your reasoning.

26 Your tolerance will be tested today as someone will irritate you because of the way they talk or conduct themselves in conversation.

27 You sense a cynical energy around someone, and no matter how hard you try to convince them of your position, it will be to no avail.

28 Restrictive employment is the universe telling you that you need to get out. Look further afield today for possible opportunities awaiting you.

29 You need to be shrewd, possibly even sneaky, to complete a job to your satisfaction. Lock yourself away before commencing it.

30 If you suspect someone of wrong-doing, you may need to arrange a silent raid to prove your point.

OCTOBER

Monthly Highlight

Important communications take place this month, and although you will be extremely busy in your work arena, it may not have much to do with the tasks at hand. Prioritise what is necessary or you may find yourself getting to the end of the month without any tangible results.

Your social activities will stimulate you this month, particularly after the 8th, when Venus comes into contact with your social zone as well as the Sun. You can expect a bright new cycle to occur in this area of your life. You may also be planning a long journey, holiday or time away from your normal routine as the New Moon enters your zone of long-distance journeys.

1 You could be in an extreme phase right now. The secret is containment. Don't give away your energies too quickly as you may need power in the coming weeks.

2 Someone with a Bible may come knocking on your door. Unless you have plenty of time to discuss philosophical differences, you may want to pretend you are not home.

3 You are keen to devise ways of saving money. It's just as well. You may find yourself somewhat overloaded with bills.

4 You are not in the least liable for an error today, but someone may be holding you responsible. You need to fight for your rights.

5 You need to be realistic about the way you fight your battles just now. Even if you win a skirmish, you may in fact lose the war.

6 You may think that someone is gentle, only to find out that they are considerably ruthless.

7 You have to be convincing in your presentation if you expect people to jump on board and support you. You need more work to achieve this.

8 You may have debts that are outside the normal range right now. You need to think carefully about prioritising your needs.

9 You could be wondering about new techniques to entice people you are attracted to. Practising the art of seduction will improve your prospects.

10 If you volunteer to champion a new cause, you need to be clear on the commitment level that is required. You may come undone if they're expecting more than you can give.

11 You need to keep things private, even if you believe someone is trustworthy. Your confidential information may be revealed in an instant when that person's guard is down.

12 If you feel awkward shopping in an expensive boutique with a friend, you should say so. You are under no compulsion to spend money if you can't afford it.

13 You'll be ill-equipped to finish your tasks on time if you scatter your energies everywhere today. Try to manage your time better.

14 If you injure the leader of your peer group, you may be shooting yourself in the foot. You need to work in a team today for the best outcome.

15 Beware the Colgate smile. Someone may be offering you an empty gesture for their own selfish gains. You could be swindled now.

16 Your imagination is excellent, but you need to apply this to the practical affairs of your life, such as paperwork, commerce and other financial matters.

17 If you're looking at expressing your thoughts or experiences on paper, you need to be motivated and disciplined on a day-by-day basis. Set aside a small amount of time to chronicle your life.

18 A powerful woman may cross your path and strike up a friendship with you today. Whatever you do today will be brilliant and captivate the imagination of others.

19 This is not a time to shrink back from situations requiring an authoritative hand. If you've been going through personal relationship conflicts and have reached the end of the line, you need to legally settle the issues.

20 Demand that your rights be met and fulfilled. You are sentimental and nostalgic about the past today, and may have an opportunity to reconnect with someone dear to you.

21 If someone is misleading you, refer them to the appropriate documentation. This will clarify the matter.

22 Loaning money to others is always fraught with danger and you may need to collect right now. This could cause some strain on a relationship.

23 Finances can be misleading and you may be reading the numbers wrongly. Double-check all maths and accounts.

24 Venus may tug at your heart strings and give you a sense of romantic connectedness with someone you work with. The habit of being with the same person is the only thing keeping you there.

25 You could meet others who help you dissolve some of your fears, boundaries or feelings of guilt and insecurity. Their compassion can inspire you to greater things.

26 You need to be convinced before changing your opinion today. The arguments just don't stack up. Suspicion is your keyword.

27 If a promise is broken, perhaps you didn't trust your instincts or you applied too much pressure. Take some time out to reassess.

28 Once again, reset the boundaries in your relationships, otherwise you may have to suffer the consequences. Ask the hard questions today.

29 You have a lucky chance today, so don't blow it by having too many things on the boil and being scattered. Focus on one thing.

30 Getting physical rest doesn't mean that your mind will follow suit. You need to learn the art of relaxation through deep breathing.

31 We usually hate bureaucracy, but when it helps us, we appreciate it fully. Today, utilise government resources to solve a problem.

NOVEMBER

Monthly Highlight

This is the time of the year when the Sun moves through the upper part of your horoscope, indicating promotions, energy, satisfaction in your work and the likelihood of great success. Don't blow it. Although you have continuing responsibilities in this particular part of your life, thanks to the slow-moving presence of Saturn, you come out ahead and achieve some wonderful results. The Sun and Jupiter enter into a perfectly wonderful triangular aspect on the 13th, indicating good fortune, luck and a long-awaited breakthrough. Another excellent aspect is when Mars and Jupiter make contact on the 20th, triggering some new activities.

---

1 A work-related event is exciting. A social event may bring you into the limelight and make you the talk of the town.

---

2 The pace picks up for you now. You are focusing more clearly on work without feeling that others are distracting you. You will initiate new projects and take the lead.

3 Even if you are opposed by others, they will not get the better of you. Yes, you will be successful in gaining an unfair advantage, but you must not alienate friends or co-workers with your dynamic energy.

4 Give consideration to what others suggest as you develop greater insight into improving your skills. What appears to be opposition might actually be a blessing in disguise.

5 Your words have more power during this phase, so schedule meetings and utilise this to your advantage. You have an opportunity to fulfil contractual desires.

6 Write your wish list, create your vision board and dare to dream big dreams. Don't be afraid to open up the vista of your ambition to what's possible.

7 Travelling and business are intimately linked. It will be a pleasant surprise, but more so if you're working in a field that gives you little flexibility to get about.

8 You will capitalise on real estate and other fixed assets. Take stock of what you possess and what you owe, but don't go into too much debt right now.

9 Tear up your credit cards. Take more control of your finances.

10 Your public relations skills are dynamic at the moment. You will win over those who have the power to improve your financial status and approval rating. Wine and dine those who have more power and affluence.

11 If you feel out of your depth at a social event, do some studies beforehand so you can feel more in tune with how the rich and famous live.

12 Although you may want a promotion just now, you may have to be patient and wait until the time is right. Rest assured that the universe runs like clockwork.

13 Don't let laziness deter you from completing and executing your ideas right now. You may have to work behind the scenes in the coming weeks.

14 Don't waste valuable energy today. Indecision is a waste of time and energy. Sometimes you need to make a decision in spite of yourself.

15 Don't let yourself be swayed by someone whose advice is not too sound. Rely on your own intuition today.

16 You have an immense drive to uncover the truth today. But you mustn't use a sledgehammer to break open a walnut. Speak calmly and patiently about what you want your lover or partner to reveal.

17 Considered pre-loved goods if you're a little strapped for cash. Your friends will be amazed at your good taste.

18 Your sexuality is strong right now, but you are being too emotional. Stop struggling and let things happen naturally.

19 If there are unsettled feelings in your relationship, talk about what is on your mind. You mustn't indulge any negativity today.

20 Slow and deliberate thinking will help avoid errors. Some tedious work may be rushed. Do it properly the first time around.

21 You may feel annoyed by someone right now, but you may not know how to tell them to get lost. It is easy—just say it!

22 A wolf in sheep's clothing will enter your social circle and it could be difficult to stop them. Look behind them to see what their footprints are like.

23 Misunderstandings will continue to occur if you don't listen. Expect a happy surprise in your work arena.

24 Your focus should not be on the frustration you've had, even if the conditions were intolerable. Use your creative mind to change the situation.

25 Try not to overlook an appointment today. You may forget some significant details that could make you look bad, or, worse still, cause you to lose money.

26 Divided loyalties could be a problem for you when one friend is set up against another. You need to remain impartial.

27 Festive events and social gatherings are favoured, so put work or serious matters on the backburner and let romance take the front seat.

28 Don't be afraid to be spontaneous and flexible in the way you approach things. Friends may not understand you, but this is your life.

29 A disappointment in your relationship may be inevitable because you are focusing too much on family problems.

30 You may be shy or afraid of some sort of confrontation. If you bury the issue, it will only explode at a later date.

DECEMBER

Monthly Highlight

A new circle of friends may come into view as you start to expand and extend your social networks. The New Moon occurs early in the month, around the 3rd, and you will feel some significant changes take place.

Venus is luxurious in the 12th zone of hidden activities, so you will be planning expenditures on artistic and cultural pursuits. This may also have to do with some secret affair or romantic activities that you prefer to keep to yourself. Overall, the last month of the year may be somewhat low-key for you, Aquarius.

1 Your co-workers and employer may be excessively demanding, and you might feel a tug of war between your duties to both.

2 Don't lean too heavily on friends as it will confuse them. If you do have to rely on someone, be upfront.

3 If you're finding it hard to handle stodgy old rules and conventions in your workplace, you've got one of two choices: adjust yourself to the prevailing conditions, or get out.

4 Your high level of mental energy could be operating in fits and starts, and this could be draining your energy reserves. Drop a few activities.

5 You could be feeling overlooked at the moment and this will play on your emotions. There's no point trying to attract others when you don't feel attractive.

6 Spontaneity seems to be a keyword for you right now. You can kick back and enjoy yourself, particularly if you've got a few friends you want to catch up with.

7 An assertive personal style is needed right now, even at the risk of treading on a few toes. Being more dramatic will get the results that you want.

8 Don't get caught up in the same old patterns with co-workers. Try a different approach today. A little reverse psychology will go a long way.

9 You're feeling confident, and doing something on the spur of the moment is tempting. Be careful; you might be let down by someone going back on their word.

10 Take the initiative in carrying out your creative ambitions. Acknowledge what needs to be changed in your surroundings.

11 You may be offered a hand in friendship, or someone who has a deeper interest in you may not be to your liking. You'll probably walk away.

12 You decide to do something on the spur of the moment, much to the surprise of your friends and loved ones. This should turn into a fun time.

13 Surprising a loved one is always a nice idea, and today is no exception. A small gift or a loving phone call will bring rewards.

14 Taking a risk seems to be the order of the day, but you can't act alone. Your plans may be thwarted.

15 You might go out somewhere only to find that the atmosphere is worse than the one you were trying to escape. Remember, accepting invitations is not obligatory.

16 Your health may not be up to par today. This could have something to do with financial concerns. Don't worry about things you cannot change.

17 Power tripping is the name of the game, and someone you work with may be exerting their authority—much to your chagrin. You need to meet them head-on to assert some level of equality in the workplace.

18 You have to support your partner or best friend because they have an opportunity to change their life. Don't question it, even if you don't quite trust what they're doing. Just be there for them.

19 You may seem a little intense and self-absorbed to those around you. Explain where you are coming from.

20 You will not be satisfied until you finish your work today. Everything has to be done in a big way, and spreading yourself too thin could cause health problems. Slow down.

21 Your positive thinking will help in some negotiation today. A new opportunity may spring up, just when you thought it was dead in the water.

22 You may lose money or misplace valuable items. Don't suspect friends; you simply misplaced the valuables.

23 A challenge from others may cause you to dig in your heels and become successful in spite of yourself.

24 You may decide to learn a foreign language or homemaking skill that could be the basis for meeting like-minded people and new friends.

25 You are oozing with commercial and financial desire right now, but you may shrug off or minimise helpful ideas that are presented to you.

26 Family members and loved ones may put additional strain on you. There will be new conditions to contend with in your domestic environment.

27 You feel inclined to gamble or play games of chance today. Be warned; the omens do not favour wasteful expenditure just now.

28 The flame of your love, or your partner's, may have dwindled lately. It's your responsibility to do what you can to recharge it.

29 You will meet a person who has so many problems in their life that you'll appreciate your own good fortune.

30 You have to reappraise your attitudes to sex, love and issues of commitment. Confusion may arise if you have to make a decision surrounding these matters.

31 There is a strong sexual attraction between you and another person at the moment, but you're definitely holding back. Don't think about it; you must act upon these impulses.

2013
ASTRONUMEROLOGY

BE NICE TO NERDS. YOU MAY
END UP WORKING FOR THEM.
WE ALL COULD.

Charles J. Sykes

THE POWER BEHIND YOUR NAME

Did you know that your name actually resonates at a certain frequency, a vibration that is unique to you? To find out what this vibration is, and how it affects you and your destiny, you simply add the numbers of your name to reveal which planet is governing you. This is an ancient form of numerology based upon the Chaldean system in which each number is assigned a planetary vibration. Take a look at the chart below to see how each alphabetical letter is connected to a planetary energy.

AIJQY	**=**	**1**	**Sun**
BKR	**=**	**2**	**Moon**
CGLS	**=**	**3**	**Jupiter**
DMT	**=**	**4**	**Uranus**
EHNX	**=**	**5**	**Mercury**
UVW	**=**	**6**	**Venus**
OZ	**=**	**7**	**Neptune**
FP	**=**	**8**	**Saturn**
—	**=**	**9**	**Mars**

Note: The number 9 is not allotted a letter because it is a mysterious vibration and considered 'unknowable'.

Once the numbers have been added together, they result in a number which is associated with a planet that rules your name and personal affairs.

It is no accident that many famous actors, writers and musicians have modified their names. They use these name changes to attract luck and good fortune, which can be facilitated by using the energies of a friendlier planet. Try experimenting with the table and see how new names affect you. It's so much fun and may even attract greater love, wealth and worldly success!

By studying the following example, you too can work out the power of your name. If your name is Andrew Brown, calculate the ruling planet by correlating each letter to a number in the table, like this:

A	**N**	**D**	**R**	**E**	**W**	**B**	**R**	**O**	**W**	**N**
1	**5**	**4**	**2**	**5**	**6**	**2**	**2**	**7**	**6**	**5**

And then add the numbers like this:

1 + 5 + 4 + 2 + 5 + 6 + 2 + 2 + 7 + 6 + 5 = 45

Then add **4 + 5 = 9**

The ruling number of Andrew Brown's name is 9, which is ruled by Mars. (See how the nine can now be used?) Now study the Name-Number Table to reveal the power of your name. The numbers 4 and 5 will play a secondary role in Andrew's character and destiny, so in this case you would also study the effects of Uranus (4) and Mercury (5).

Your Name Number	Ruling Planet	Your Name Characteristics
1	Sun	Beautiful character. Able to sway people with their charm. Physically active. They enjoy sports and other competitive activities. Many friends and rich and wealthy well-wishers. Excellent connections in government circles and with political individuals. Makes a wonderful friend. Can be loyal but stubborn.
2	Moon	Soft, receptive and emotional by nature. Extreme change of moods. Highly sensitive and psychic. Curious nature, kind-hearted and creative in many areas. Strong love of family and friends. Prefers night to day. Women have a strong karmic influence on them.

Your Name Number	Ruling Planet	Your Name Characteristics
3	Jupiter	Strong philosophical nature. Supreme optimist but at times opportunistic, which is unnecessary because a great deal of luck is associated with Jupiter. Great sense of timing. Expansive and generous nature that may be wasteful at times. Travel will bring them many interesting experiences.
4	Uranus	Unusual character with an erratic nature. Unusual likes and dislikes. Many unexpected experiences, ups and downs and interesting but short-lived relationships. May become bored easily and needs to plan more carefully for a stable life.
5	Mercury	Master communicator. A love of change and variety which may lead to an ever-shifting pattern of life without stability. Always young at heart, playful and attractive to all. Attracted to the written and spoken word. Quick witted.

Your Name Number	Ruling Planet	Your Name Characteristics
6	Venus	Seductive and delightful personality. Gracious and social by nature. Eye-catching personality with a variety of friends. Expert in bedroom arts and also able to make money through social activities. Music, art and other aesthetic activities take pride of place in life. Strong family ties that need to be carefully balanced with career appetites.
7	Neptune	One of the most spiritual numbers, which indicates a psychic and self-sacrificing nature. Unconditional in love and able to develop the most altruistic character. Prophetic, a dreamer, but sometimes victimised by the very people they wish to help. Can be a romantic idealist.

Your Name Number	Ruling Planet	Your Name Characteristics
8	Saturn	An excessively hard worker, sometimes overly preoccupied by money and security. Great powers of concentration. Will usually work long and hard to achieve ambitions. Slow in giving trust and demands perfection in all areas of life. Sometimes overly serious, but a loyal character.
9	Mars	Immense stamina and recuperative powers. Highly physical and sexual individual. Often steamrolls others, but means well. Combative, competitive, arrogant and playful. Injury-prone. Protects family and is extremely loyal to all he or she considers important. Great success through sheer effort.

YOUR PLANETARY RULER

Astrology and numerology are very closely aligned. Each planet rules over a number between 1 and 9. Both your name and your birth date are ruled by planetary energies. Here are the planets and their ruling numbers:

1	**Sun**
2	**Moon**
3	**Jupiter**
4	**Uranus**
5	**Mercury**
6	**Venus**
7	**Neptune**
8	**Saturn**
9	**Mars**

To find out which planet will control the coming year for you, simply add the numbers of your birth date and the year in question. Here is an example:

If you were born on 12 November, add the numerals 1 and 2 (12, your day of birth) and 1 and 1 (11, your month of birth) to the year in question, in this case 2013 (current year), like this:

Add 1 + 2 + 1 + 1 + 2 + 0 + 1 + 3	**=**	**11**
1 + 1	**=**	**2**

The planet ruling your individual karma for 2013 will be the Moon because this planet rules the number 2.

YOUR PLANETARY FORECAST

You can even take your ruling name number, as discussed previously, and add it to the year in question to throw more light on your coming personal affairs, like this:

A N D R E W B R O W N	**=**	**9**
Year coming	**=**	**2013**
Add 9 + 2 + 0 + 1 + 3	**=**	**15**
Add 1 + 5	**=**	**6**

This is the ruling year number using your name number as a basis. You would then study the influence of Venus (6) for 2013. Good luck!

Trends for Your Planetary Number in 2013

Year Number	Ruling Planet	Results Throughout the Coming Year
1	Sun	**Overview** The commencement of a new cycle: a year full of accomplishments, increased reputation, brand new plans and projects. New responsibilities, success and strong physical vitality. Health should improve and illnesses will be healed. If you have ailments, this is the time to improve your physical wellbeing—recovery will be certain. **Love and pleasure** A lucky year for love. Credit connection with children. Family life is in focus. Music, art and creative expression will be fulfilling. New romantic opportunities. **Work** Minimal effort for maximum luck. Extra money and exciting professional opportunities. Positive new changes result in promotion and pay rises. **Improving your luck** Luck is plentiful, particularly in July and August. The 1st, 8th, 15th and 22nd hours of Sundays are lucky. Your lucky numbers are 1, 10, 19 and 28.

Year Number	Ruling Planet	Results Throughout the Coming Year
2	Moon	**Overview** Reconnection with your emotions and past. Excellent for relationships with family members. Moodiness may become a problem. Sleeping patterns will be affected. **Love and pleasure** Home, family life and relationships are in focus this year. Relationships improve through self-effort and greater communication. Change of residence, renovations and interior decoration bring satisfaction. Increased psychic sensitivity. **Work** Emotional in work. Home career, or hobby from a domestic base, will bring greater income opportunities. Females will be more prominent in your work. **Improving your luck** July will fulfil some of your dreams. Monday will be lucky with the 1st, 8th, 15th and 22nd hours being particularly fortunate. Pay special attention to the New and Full Moons in 2013. Your lucky numbers include 2, 11, 20, 29 and 38.

Year Number	Ruling Planet	Results Throughout the Coming Year
3	Jupiter	**Overview** A lucky year for you. Exciting opportunities will expand your horizons. Good fortune financially. Travels and increased popularity. A happy year. Your spiritual inclinations will grow and you will also want to explore the world. Travel is on the cards. **Love and pleasure** You feel confident about romance during this cycle. You may meet someone during busy activity or while travelling. This is a good opportunity to deepen your love for your partner. **Work** Fortunate for new opportunities and success. Employers are more accommodating and open to your creative expression. Extra money. New job promotions are possible.. **Improving your luck** Remain realistic, get more sleep and don't expect too much from your efforts. Planning is necessary for better luck. The 1st, 8th, 15th and 24th hours of Thursdays are spiritually very lucky for you.

Year Number	Ruling Planet	Results Throughout the Coming Year
3	Jupiter	Your lucky numbers are 3, 12, 21, and 30. March and December are lucky months. 2013 will bring you some unexpected surprises.

Year Number	Ruling Planet	Results Throughout the Coming Year
4	Uranus	**Overview** Don't take things for granted during this cycle as changes may occur when you least expect them. Unexpected twists and turns of fate. Possibility of having to begin all over again. Progressive attitude may bring many unusual and uplifting experiences. **Love and pleasure** Guard against dissatisfaction in relationships. You require plenty of freedom and experimentation. Love may take you by surprise. You could meet someone when you least expect it, but the relationship may turn out to be tumultuous. **Work** Unusual and modern lines of work are likely in the coming year and you need to be open to new ideas to enhance your career prospects. Working with technological apparatus, software and other online tools will be of interest to you. Try not to overwork and find ways to reduce your stress levels.

Year Number	Ruling Planet	Results Throughout the Coming Year
4	Uranus	**Improving your luck** Temperance is your keyword in the coming 12 months. Be patient and do not rush things. Slow your pace this year as impulse will only lead to errors and missed opportunities. Exercise greater patience in all matters. Steady investments are lucky. The 1st, 8th, 15th and 20th hours of any Saturday will be very lucky for you in 2013. Your lucky numbers are 4, 13, 22 and 31.

Year Number	Ruling Planet	Results Throughout the Coming Year
5	Mercury	**Overview** You are moving so quickly that things appear to be in fast-forward mode. You need to pace yourself, even if your imagination and communication skills are at a peak. New ideas will fascinate you and life will seem full of opportunities. Intellectual activities and communications increase. Your imagination is powerful. New and exciting ideas will bring success and personal satisfaction. **Love and pleasure** Relationships take on a more playful air in 2013. You must be adaptable to keep pace with your family members and your own schedule. Love affairs may be confusing as you could become indecisive. Try to accept your spouse or partner for who they are. You may become critical. Learn to curb your impulse to find fault. **Work** Your innovative ideas put you ahead of your work peers. You will meet many people and may also develop an interest in commerce and finance. You will want to trade and increase profitability in your business.

Year Number	Ruling Planet	Results Throughout the Coming Year
5	Mercury	You can achieve a senior position if you are prepared to assume additional responsibilities. Don't do too much. Speed, efficiency and capability are your keywords this year. Don't be impulsive in making a career change. Travel is also on your agenda. **Improving your luck** Write down your ideas, research topics more thoroughly, and communicate your enthusiasm through meetings. This will afford you much more luck. Stick to one idea. The 1st, 8th, 15th and 20th hours of Wednesday are luckiest, so schedule your meetings and other important social engagements at these times. Your lucky numbers are 5, 14, 23 and 32.

Year Number	Ruling Planet	Results Throughout the Coming Year
6	Venus	**Overview** 2013 will be an important year for romance and new relationships. You will be sensual as well as sexually self-indulgent. Your family affairs will take precedence over other aspects of your life. You may want to work with the one you love. Money should be plentiful, but only if you reduce your overheads and unnecessary expenses. **Love and pleasure** Your keyword in the next 12 months is romance. An existing romance is deepened now. You may meet someone new who can help you develop greater self-esteem. You will take on a new look. Put your best foot forward. Engagement, or even marriage, is quite possible. Increase in social responsibilities. Moderate your excessive tendencies. **Work** Your protective instincts and desire for greater future security will dominate your working life. You will be finding ways to cut back costs and save more money. Combining your professional and domestic life is also likely. Working from home may be preferable.

Year Number	Ruling Planet	Results Throughout the Coming Year
6	Venus	**Improving your luck** Work and success are dependent on your creative and positive mental attitude. Eliminate bad habits and personality tendencies that can obstruct you. Balance spiritual and financial needs. The 1st, 8th, 15th and 20th hours on Fridays are extremely lucky for you this year and new opportunities can arise when you least expect it. The numbers 6, 15, 24 and 33 will generally increase your luck.

Year Number	Ruling Planet	Results Throughout the Coming Year
7	Neptune	**Overview** This is an intuitive and spiritually karmic year. Your life goals become more focused, but you need to rely on your inner resources to get you across the line. You need to be careful of people who might use you this year. Don't be too trusting. **Love and pleasure** You may meet someone who is your spiritual soul mate this year. Your love is idealistic and you will not settle for anything less than perfect. You may put people on pedestals because you are not seeing their character clearly. Try to look at people truthfully. **Work** You may wish to become involved in humanitarian work or get involved in activities that can help you foster your spiritual ideals. Clearing out your environment of negative vibrations will help you focus and become more successful. Use your intuition in any job move. Your hunches will be correct.

Year Number	Ruling Planet	Results Throughout the Coming Year
7	Neptune	**Improving your luck** Be very clear in what you are trying to communicate and stick to one path this year for best results. Pay attention to your health and don't let this stress affect your positive outlook. Sleep well, exercise and develop better eating habits to allow greater energy circulation. The 1st, 8th, 15th and 20th hours of Wednesday are your luckiest, so schedule your meetings and other important social engagements at these times. Your lucky numbers are 5, 14, 23 and 32.

Year Number	Ruling Planet	Results Throughout the Coming Year
8	Saturn	**Overview** You have passed previous tests in life and should now be strong enough to deal with anything that life throws at you. You need to be practical and pay attention to traditional structures, and other conservative requirements. You could become a workaholic, so pace yourself and make sure your diary is not jam-packed. Finances should improve through your efforts. **Love and pleasure** Try not to be too serious about your relationships and keep the fun alive. Don't be too demanding and balance your professional and domestic life to keep loved ones happy. Dedicate time to your family, not just work. Schedule activities outdoors to increase your wellbeing and emotional satisfaction. **Work** Money is your focus throughout 2013, but this will require hard work on your part. You may need to make some hard decisions that could cost you friends as you choose security over outdated relationships.

Year Number	Ruling Planet	Results Throughout the Coming Year
8	Saturn	**Improving your luck** Being too cautious may cause you to miss opportunities during the coming 12 months. If new opportunities are offered, balance your head and your heart when drawing conclusions. You may be reluctant to attempt something new. Be kind to yourself and don't overwork or overdo exercise. The 1st, 8th, 15th and 20th hours of Saturdays are the best times for you in 2013. Your lucky numbers are 1, 8, 17, 26 and 35.

Year Number	Ruling Planet	Results Throughout the Coming Year
9	Mars	**Overview** In a 9 year, you will see old chapters closing and new ones opening. This may not be an easy cycle as you transition to bigger and better things. Remain open and don't hold onto the past. Do not be impulsive or irritable. Avoid arguments. Calm communication will help find solutions. **Love and pleasure** You have strong sexual impulses during this cycle. You will enjoy your sexual intimacy. Romance is dependent on personal wellbeing, so do loads of exercise to keep fit. Receptive understanding of your lovers will bring about a new and improved state of affairs. Listen carefully to your partner's needs and try to fulfil them. **Work** This is the year when your drive and industry will provide you with excellent results. There are bigger and better things on the horizon and you will actively make them happen. You are likely to take on a leadership role and receive respect and honour from others—as long as you are fair in your dealings with them.

Year Number	Ruling Planet	Results Throughout the Coming Year
9	Mars	**Improving your luck** Find an outlet for your high level of energy through meditation, self-reflection and prayer. Collect your energies and focus them on one point. Release tension to maintain health. The 1st, 8th, 15th and 20th hours of Tuesday will be lucky for you throughout 2013. Your lucky numbers are 9, 18, 27 and 36.